Speak *Up*! Speak *Out*!

Acting Techniques That Make Public Speaking *Fun* and *Fearless*!

ALSO BY KATHRYN MARIE BILD:

NON-FICTION:
> *Acting From a Spiritual Perspective*
> *The Actor's Quotation Book*

FICTION:
> *Miss Madeline Goes Shopping*
> *Uncle Ethel*
> *Einstein for Infants* (Humor)

Speak *Up*! Speak *Out*!

Acting Techniques That Make Public Speaking *Fun* and *Fearless*!

Kathryn Marie Bild

Smith and Kraus Publishers   2014

ISBN 1-57525-890-0
ISBN 978-1-57525-890-4
Library of Congress Control Number: 2014936834

Typesetting and layout by Elizabeth E. Monteleone
Cover by Borderlands Press

A Smith and Kraus book
177 Lyme Road, Hanover, NH 03755
editorial 603.643.6431 To Order 877.668.8680
www.smithandkraus.com

For Aunt Tam

ACKNOWLEDGMENTS

My deepest thanks to my publishers, Marisa Smith and Eric Kraus, who have continued to believe in me over the years and who trusted me enough to give me the go ahead on this book after my presentation to them of just the concept and a half page description, because that was all I had at the moment apart from the strong feeling that the idea had legs and would develop into something useful. I hope that it has! I thank you both for your invaluable support and your patience.

Big thanks also to Elizabeth E. Monteleone for her creativity and hard work in designing this book, to Lawrence Harbison for his insightful work as my editor, and to Carol Boynton for her work in the book's production. It would have been a much less beautiful and accessible book without their help.

Thank you to my friend and agent, Janet Rosen, who makes things happen and keeps them moving, and to my friends and family who have supported me throughout the writing of this book. Especially Katherine Gotshall English, Diana Altman, Grace Gallo, Diane Allison, Tamara Bild and Mark Holmes. Thank you, too, to my students and clients, whom I consider it an honor to coach.

TABLE OF CONTENTS

When I was eighteen, my boyfriend asked me if I would be his scene partner in a scene he was using for an audition for Paramount Pictures. I was to learn my lines then stand with my back to the director who would be looking past me at my boyfriend while he auditioned for the part. No big deal for me, no pressure. I said yes, I would give it a shot—*Paramount*, how *fun*! I memorized my lines, we practiced a few times, then the next morning we drove onto the Paramount lot, walked into the casting office, and that is the last memory I have of the entire experience until we were back outside in the parking lot. I completely blacked out the whole experience in the casting office, I was so terrified! It wasn't *fun* at all! I found, in fact, from that experience and a few others that followed, that—at that time in my life, anyway—any kind of acting, speaking, or other presentation performance was anything *but* "fun and fearless;" it was torturous and horribly *fear-filled*.

My boyfriend told me that I'd done all right. I got the words out at the right time and I didn't do anything particularly wrong (he didn't get the part, by the way). But I'd done no preparation for the role beyond just memorizing the words, which I'd thought was enough. I discovered when I was on the hot seat and it came time to perform, however, that it wasn't.

Subsequent to my day of terror, I took up the study of acting for a few years and then I began to teach it. I've been teaching acting for over twenty years, now—classes, workshops, and private coaching. In addition to discovering years ago that an actor actually needs to know—beyond just memorizing—what he or she is doing when making a theatrical speech(!), I have recently made another discovery, this one even more important because it is so much farther reaching in its usefulness. I have discovered that the acting techniques that I have been employing for years to help my acting students master and deliver beautifully-honed, well-controlled theatrical speeches can also be used to help public speakers and other presenters master and deliver *any* kind of speech. And there are so many kinds of speeches and so many opportunities to make them every day. I find this very exciting! Think of the possibilities, the vastness of resource! Millions—*Billions*—of people, each one with such rich, unique insight to share. And they, like we, share more readily when they've developed the skill—and the confidence that comes with it—to do so.

This idea started to dawn on me when a friend of mine asked me to coach her in making her "mother of the bride" speech at her daughter's wedding. We approached the speech as if it was a theatrical monologue, and we worked with various acting techniques until she felt strong and in control. And she was a smash at the wedding! Then others came along. A businesswoman asked for techniques to calm and steady her nerves when making a report to her company's shareholders. An association president wanted to come off as "more masterful." I called upon tried and true acting techniques to help them, and these time-honored techniques did help them! Then I began giving workshops and seminars on the topic, and attendees found my discovery to be valid—good, strong acting techniques do help make public speaking and presenting more effective, as well as more fun and fearless on the part of the presenter! Then they said, "Write a book," so here I am.

We are going to be taking a look at what speaking is, what makes a good speaker, how to define yourself as a speaker and what to speak about when it is in your control to make that choice. But we are going to be dealing more with the delivery or performance of a speech than with constructing its content. And yet, since it is so that "In the beginning was the word," do be clear that if the content is not there, no delivery, no matter how proficient, is going to make something out of nothing.

There are acting tips and affirmations throughout the book that I hope will inspire and encourage you in your work as a speaker. And, more important for your progress, there are acting exercises, which I strongly urge you to perform. At least some of them. As we all know, it's the hands-on doing it that gets it done in life. Besides, I think you'll enjoy them.

The main purpose of this book is to help you gain mastery, so that you will be able to go confidently into any arena, no matter the type or size, and be able to say whatever you have to say without resistance or fear of any kind, so that we—your audience—may benefit by your unique contribution. I hope you will find that the techniques herein help you to do that. Thank you for letting me share them with you.

PART ONE

"The Magnificent Art of Public Speaking"

CHAPTER ONE

The Universal Impulse to Speak

"All the world's a stage...and one man in his time plays many parts."

— *As You Like It* by William Shakespeare

"Birds do it. Bees do it. Even educated fleas do it." Fall in love? Yes. And then they *speak up and speak out* about it! Birds chirp happily, bees buzz with this and other news; fleas, I'm not so sure. But they do seem ubiquitous, don't they? Especially to their host, the hound dog, who is "crying all the time!" And they do seem to be in communication about something! And why not? "Oh, what a beautiful morning! Oh, what a beautiful day! I've got a beautiful feeling...!" That in itself would be enough, but listen as *Oklahoma's* Curly tells you what his feeling is, for he yearns to tell us: "Everything's going my way!" Magnificent! Can you blame him for wanting to share his great feeling with us? For "shouting the good news from the housetop?" He can't help it! He cannot resist. Neither can the birds or the bees, or the fleas. Nor hound dogs with sadder tales, fueled by just as powerful urges to share them. Nor can the rest of us—you and I—who have so much to say and such powerful impetus to say it!

Why can't we resist? Why must we speak? "That's just the way life is," some would answer. True, but *why*, we persist? Why do we feel impelled to tell of our joy and tell of our sorrow, to sing out praises and sing the blues? Why must we communicate with one another, share our knowledge, "speak our piece" at a rally, say something to make someone laugh?

Could it be that we have the urge to communicate, the urge to speak, because it is the nature of "truth" to make itself known, through everyone? That everyone is a mouthpiece for the truth? If so, then everybody has something to say. Something true. And unique to him. And useful to others. That's why there's always room for another book.

Sometimes I go into Barnes and Noble and stare at the seemingly billions upon billions of books there and I get small and I think, "Do people really need another book, a book by *me*?" And then I realize, of course they do, for the very reason that it *is* my book. And we need your books, and your lectures and workshops, and your speeches. And your points of view. We're here on Earth on purpose. It's not a fluke. And *since you are here,* your point of view is not only to be counted, it is needed. And it is to our collective benefit, as a society, that you feel the impulse to share it with us.

ACTING TIP:
DEVELOP SELF-AFFIRMING INNER MONOLOGUES

ALL "SPEECHES" ARE SPEECHES

What comes to mind when you think the word "speech"? So and so is giving a *speech*? Is it a big speech, like a political speech or an address or a lecture? Or a summation given by an attorney to a jury? Maybe it's a speech given by an inspirational/motivational speaker. Or a spokesperson for a particular product. Then again, it might be a very short and simple speech such as an introduction or a short announcement, which could turn out to be the most appreciated speech of the day: "Ladies and gentlemen, the bathrooms are over there!" Or, perhaps, one is called on to lead a prayer, or make a toast. There are many types of speeches, each one delineated primarily by its purpose. But whatever the type of speaking opportunity or task of the speech—whether the speech is personal or business, whether you originate it yourself or you, the speaker, like an actor, are called upon strictly to deliver it—they all have one thing in common: they are all speeches. As such, they are united by common performance and presentation challenges and can all, therefore, benefit by the application of certain proven acting techniques that have helped actors with their presentations for over one hundred years.

THE TYPES OF SPEECHES

Let's get an overview of some of the different types of speeches given today, before we begin to apply to them the acting techniques that will help you make them come alive! I've put together a list of twenty-some types. There are others but this is a good cross section:

Making an announcement	Giving a report
Making a sales pitch	Being on a panel
Participating in an interview	Being a spokesperson
Giving a legal argument/summation	Making a toast
Making an introduction	Serving as host or hostess at a dinner party
Telling a story or a joke	Reading aloud
Conducting a workshop	Making a political speech
Speaking out against an injustice	Being a talk show host
Giving a lecture	Giving an address
Giving a sermon	Giving an inspirational/motivational talk
Leading a prayer	Doing stand-up
Singing a song	Giving a theatrical speech

Notice that I have listed these types or kinds of speeches randomly, with no attempt to prioritize them according to "importance," or to alphabetize them. That is because what might not be important to one speaker giving one kind of speech may be very important to another giving another. Also, most of us will give several types of speeches throughout our careers and personal experience, and the challenges, and the opportunities to meet and master those challenges, apply to all of them. One learning experience informs the next, no matter the order. No speech is too small, and no concern too unimportant to be dismissed as insignificant to this effort.

A GROUPING BY TYPES

Here is the list of the types of speeches again, categorized for the sake of easier reference.

THE BIGGER/LONGER SPEECHES	BUSINESS SPEECHES
Political/political activist	Making a presentation or report
An address	Being on a panel
Inspirational/ motivational	Making a sales pitch
Legal argument/ summation	Giving or conducting an interview
	Being a spokesperson

INSTRUCTIONAL SPEECHES	PERFORMANCE SPEECHES
Giving a lecture or sermon	Theatrical
Conducting a workshop	Stand Up
	Talk show hosting
	Reading aloud

SMALLER/SHORTER SPEECHES

Making an introduction or announcement
Leading a prayer or a song
Making a toast
Telling a story or a joke
Serving as host/hostess at a dinner party

THE VARIOUS VENUES

Where do you give these speeches? The many different speeches listed above may each be given or delivered in a variety of different venues—some in one or two, some in several. Here is a sample list of venues. Take a moment and imagine which speeches might be delivered in which venues, won't you? Be creative.

Auditoriums	Gymnasiums	Halls
Town halls	Hotels	Clubs
Stores	Conference centers	Conference rooms
Boardrooms	Night clubs	Schools
College campuses	Theatres	TV stations
Studios	Museums	Parks
Association meeting rooms	Homes	Churches/Temples/Mosques

THE OPULENT "OPPORTUNITY"

Again, randomly listed. But look at the *Opportunity*! It's amazing, isn't it? So many ways to speak and so many venues in which to do so. My hope is that these lists will inspire you, prime the pump for you, and remind—or inform—you how important it is to your success—professionally and personally—to be able to "speak well."

In the recent film, *William and Kate*— about the betrothal between the English prince and his bride to be—William's grandmother, Queen Elizabeth, played by actress Jane Alexander, asks Kate, "Have you done much public speaking?" Kate says no. Referring to her father's (King George's) struggle to overcome a severe speech impediment—so brilliantly depicted in another recent film, *The King's Speech*, by Colin Firth—Elizabeth concludes by saying, "We all must do our part." That sense of duty—that we all must do our part—is a great aid in helping the speaker grow into his or her destiny.

WHY DON'T WE TAKE THE OPPORTUNITY?

Not only do we all have many opportunities to speak publicly during our lives, we have many more opportunities than we will ever take. Why is that? Yes, we're busy in today's world, terribly busy. But I don't think that's why. I think we "sit this one out," and the next one, because we don't feel certain that we can achieve the task well. I am happy to tell you that that is going to change as you keep reading this book. Not only are the techniques and other ideas offered in the following pages going to help you radically amp your performances, you are going to more readily recognize opportunities to speak when they present themselves to you. You'll hear or see something, and you'll think, "Something needs to be said about that." You don't have to act on that, though, of course, but you may decide to. At the very least, you will know that you are able to do so. And that will make you more of a player in this magnificent world of ours that is shaped by our participation in it.

> **ACTING TIP:**
> KEEP A JOURNAL OF "IMPORTANT POINTS"
> THAT OCCUR TO YOU THROUGHOUT YOUR DAY.

MAY I BE YOUR COACH?

Please allow me to be your very own personal speech coach as you proceed through these pages! And what I, as your coach, want for you—whether you're addressing the PTA or the UN, or your neighbor over the back fence or your spouse, is for you to cultivate a greater sense of confidence and fearlessness when you tell your truth. I want you *to* tell your truth, number one; and I want you to tell it with greater confidence. I'll help you get to the point where you can do that. Then *you* decide when and where to do so. This talent, this skill to speak well, is a right of everyone. And it can be developed.

> ### *affirmation:*
>
> We are all stars.
> And Life needs each one of
> us to shine fully in order to
> be fully aglitter!

TWO MORE LISTS

In addition to the lists of the types of speeches one might make and the various venues in which one might make them, here are two more—much shorter—lists to help orient you on your path to becoming a powerful speaker.

The first addresses the important question: "Why do we give speeches at all?" What motivates people to stand at the head of a long conference table, or at a dining room table, take to the podium, sit on a panel, or step up and stand out in a crowd? The consensus reached among those who have studied these things over the years is that there are four main reasons why speeches are given. Put another way, every speech has one of four main purposes. What are they?

THE FOUR MAIN PURPOSES OF SPEECHES

> To Inform
> To Inspire (or congratulate or praise)
> To Entertain
> To Persuade

Every speech has, as its underpinning, one of these four main purposes. Theoretically. In practice, nearly every speech has a combination of two or more purposes. For example, giving a sermon may have the purpose of inspiring but it may also be meant to persuade its listeners to re-join the fold. Making a toast may be meant to congratulate but also to entertain. Making a political speech may have the main purpose of persuading, but it may also be meant to inform and inspire. A combo or not, you, the speaker, need to be clear about the reasons you are giving a particular speech so that you can keep your eye on that goal as you proceed, and achieve it.

THE FOUR MAIN MODES OF DELIVERY OF SPEECHES

In addition to there being four main purposes of speeches, there are four main modes of delivery of those speeches—the ways we present them. In order of difficulty—and spontaneous creativity—they are:

> Manuscript Reading
> Memorized Recitation
> Extemporaneous
> Impromptu

The first mode of delivery, and the easiest, is that of reading a manuscript. No memorization—certainly no dependence upon your mind for spontaneous creativity—is necessary. Just the ability to read, a good reading technique, a little bit of practice so that you know what you're saying as you read it, plus the ability to stay calm and focused—this will see you through a decent manuscript reading.

The second mode of delivery, memorized recitation, relies very much on your memory but, like memorized acting parts, will only be *good* if it is delivered with the appropriate meaning, so that you know what you are saying and you are saying it the way that you mean it—which is a result of thorough preparation.

The third main mode of delivery of a speech is extemporaneous speaking. It works like this: you have a general idea of what you want to talk about—a topic and a reason for speaking—and maybe a couple of notes or a brief outline, written or memorized, and then you let her rip. You rely on the moment and the audience participation. You know where you are heading but you allow the speech to unfold as you present it. This is as "impromptu" and as brave as most people get, but it is not truly impromptu.

Impromptu speaking, the fourth mode of delivery, is the most difficult and, I think, the most pure mode of delivery of a speech, or of public speaking. Many think impromptu speaking is the same as extemporaneous speaking but it isn't. Extemporaneous speaking has a little bit of prep to it, whereas impromptu does not. "Impromptu" means, you're standing around at a gathering of some sort and somebody says, "Hey, Bob, will you say a few words?" Or you're out in the field, on the streets, and you feel the impulse to stand up on behalf of someone, or against an injustice. As with the other three modes, this one can drive, or be applied to, any *type* of speech, delivered for any *reason*; but this *mode* of delivery is completely off the cuff, fuelled purely by creative inspiration on the part of the speaker.

A LITTLE RE-CAP

We have many types of speeches that are delivered in many different venues for four main reasons via four main modes of delivery. And this is going on all over the world, all day long. Good. This gives us a good overview, and it grounds us; it brings order to our concepts of what public speaking is and the forms it can take. In essence, we participate in the practice of public speaking because it is natural to us to do so as truth-tellers. Just look at the origin of theatre and its function in society.

THE ORIGIN OF THEATRE

There are two main theories about how the theatre began. The first is that it began as a ritual to appease the gods and gain their favor—for good harvest, good fertility, victory over their enemies. The second theory is that story-telling (truth-telling) is and always has been natural and instinctive to us and that we tell our stories to make sense of our experiences, and to help others. In that order. Modern drama is just a more sophisticated way of accomplishing those same ends. It is interesting to note that both theater and speaking in public have always existed as parts of society. Neither is a luxury. They are both non-expendable functions of a healthy society.

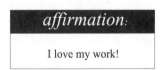

affirmation:

I love my work!

ACTING AND SELLING ARE NOT THE SAME THING

Sometimes when I tell someone who works in sales that I am an acting coach, he or she will laugh and say, "Boy, I act all day long!" He is implying that he puts on a false face to his customers, and pretends. Worse, that he is phony, insincere. *Worse*, that he is dishonest. But that's not what acting is, and it certainly isn't what public speaking is about. Yes, there is pretense in acting but only the circumstances are pretended—and everybody knows that they are; the ideas and emotions are real.

NEITHER ARE *ACTING AND PUBLIC SPEAKING* THE SAME THING

There are also some big differences between acting and public speaking. Drama's story, with its characterization and plot, is euphemistic and symbolic, representational. It is a matrix for the message. Speaking, on the other hand, is the very message itself. Not *couched* in meaning; it *is* the meaning, clearly stated. Not representative of truth, but truth itself. It is not symbolic of what you have to say; it *is* what you have to say. And yet, acting and public speaking are sister arts, both of which depend on presentation skills for their successful communication. Fortunately for those of us who practice the art of public speaking, the practitioners of her sister art have developed a group of techniques over the past one hundred years that have proven to make not only their own presentations more effective but ours—if we use them—as well.

Before we get into what they are and how to use them, though, let's look a little deeper into just exactly who we mean by "we." Who is "the speaker?"

SUMMARY OF MAIN POINTS

1. We are naturally impelled to *speak up* and *speak out.* It is one way that nature expresses herself, that truth makes itself known.
2. Everyone has something important to say, something unique to each of us.
3. We speak out through a variety of types of "speeches," which are more effective when supported by tried and true dramatic acting techniques.
4. It is very important to our success—in our professional and in our personal lives—to be able to speak well.
5. People have many more opportunities to speak than they take because they don't feel certain they can achieve the task well. But the skill to speak well can be developed.
6. Our urge to self-express as truth-tellers has always been the underpinning of the art of drama. We tell our stories to make sense of our experience.
7. Good acting represents the truth; good speaking *is* the truth. The practitioners of both arts face many of the same challenges of presentation. For this reason, techniques that have been developed to help actors are effective in helping public speakers as well.

CHAPTER TWO

Who's Speaking, Please?

"In the end, the story will sink or swim on . . . what *you*
bring to the story—what *only* you can bring to the story."

— Bob Reiss

WHO ARE "YOU?"

Who is this speaker, this *you who has something to say*?
Anyone on his way to hear a speech wants to know, first of
all, who the speaker is, because it is from who the speaker
is that his speech, in any of its many forms, emerges. That
won't remain a mystery for long, in any case, however.
Whether you are a "rock star politician" a stadium preacher
or a member of your building's co-op board about to speak
on the condition of your sprinkling system, every time you
open your mouth you tell the rest of us who you are. *You* tell
us who is speaking.

This fact reflects nicely the theory—the rule, in fact—in
the world of drama that "character determines plot," rather
than the other way around. With which I concur. The type
of person you are determines what you will do, and say. Although these things are not entirely black and white.

"I AM"

The most eloquent message I have ever heard expressed,
in content and delivery, is the well-known two short words
statement, "I am." It is stunning in its simplicity as well as in
its precision. "I am." Short and sweet. Self-declaration. Self-
affirmation. "I am." "I exist and I express my self-existence."
All the rest are details. Literally. Whether you are a sales
person, a lecturer, or an attorney, you are doing the same
thing each time you stand up to speak. You are proclaiming

your existence and you are expressing your objectives—your nature—at least insofar as it relates to your speech at hand. "Who's speaking, please?" I am.

EXERCISE:

List six good qualities that you are known for. No false modesty, please.

1. _____

2. _____

3. _____

4. _____

5. _____

6. _____

DECIDING AND BEING CERTAIN

The actor knows this. Before the actor learns his character's lines—his speech or speeches—he first sets to work to decide who this character is. *Decide*, not discover. The playwright gives him major clues in the form of a blueprint: some explanation, statements made about his character by the other characters, his character's dialogue, and, of course, the plot, or story. But the actor doesn't know how to say those words—what he wants to really mean by them—until he allows his character to form as a personality in his mind. In *his* mind, not the playwright's; as *he* sees him. What is his character's background, motivation, and desires, which have combined to make him who he is, which, in turn, causes him to think and speak and behave in certain ways? And when the actor finally decides—creates—who his character is, the words his character speaks and the way he delivers them must be found to be consistent with his personality, or we, the audience, will think something is wrong. And we'll be right.

"I AM AUTHENTIC" IN PUBLIC SPEAKING

In the world of drama, the "I" takes on characterization. "I am" a twenty-five year old man raised in Alabama, with a gambling habit, who wants to kick it in order to be allowed to spend time with my five year old daughter. "I am" a fifty year old grammar school teacher who has fallen in love for the first time and feels conflicted between starting a new life at the expense of the old one.

In the world of public speaking, "I am" me. "I am" I. *You*, the speaker, are the character. All speech, all truth, flows directly from you, with no characterization or imaginary circumstances to adopt or filter through on its way to its audience. You are yourself, *your* self. That is your authority. You have a task at hand—your reason for speaking—and you have your objectives or goals. Those things constitute the "characterization" of you, the speaker, for that particular "speech." They constitute the character you are "playing" with regards to that speech.

Whether we are playing a character on the stage, or being a speaker at the podium, what we are striving for is that our characterization is authentic. And if we have achieved that authenticity of character, it will follow, "as the night the day," that our speech will be a speech of integrity.

> **ACTING TIP:** HAVE A CLEAR VISION.

THE QUALITIES OF A GOOD SPEAKER

What qualities of character and talent make up a good speaker? Let's first ask ourselves, what are some of the qualities that make a good actor? Got your pencil ready?

EXERCISE: "Ten Qualities of a Great Speaker."

PART ONE:

Write down ten qualities that you think would be part of the makeup of a good actor.

1. _____

2. _____

3. _____

4. _____

5. _____

6. _____

7. _____

8. _____

9. _____

10. _____

Did you list any of the following qualities?

insight	compassion	understanding	love
humility	devotion	kindness	sincerity
courage	versatility	imagination	discipine
conviction	committment	dedication	humor

I'm not surprised. Hold that thought and let's go on to part two.

PART TWO:

List ten qualities you think would be part of the makeup of an individual who was a good speaker.

1. _____

2. _____

3. _____

4. _____

5. _____

6. _____

7. _____

8. _____

9. _____

10._____

Did you list any of the following?

dynamic	fearless	dependable	smart
strong	honest	vital	spontaneous
wise	rational	non-reactive	steady
well-informed	well-read	joyful	confident
passionate	easy-going	tough	clear
accurate	poised	elegant	dignified
stable	balanced	attractive	neat
powerful	visionary		

Now analyze your two lists, and consider the following questions. Could you have selected qualities from your first list, qualities of a good actor, to also be qualities of a good speaker? And vice versa? Wouldn't the audiences of both the actor and the speaker want their artists and speakers to possess the qualities on both lists? Don't we all want all of those qualities to be present in our friends and family members, and lovers? Don't we want them to be present *in ourselves*?

The good news is, they are. Each of us possesses all of those good qualities—from both lists! It is up to each of us to develop them, of course. But if the actor didn't have all of these qualities in his own psychic library he wouldn't be able to draw on them to compose a character. Because he assembles the elements of his characters from his one and only resource, himself. He would be limited, then, to playing only certain kinds of people whose components did not out-total his own. And if you, the speaker, weren't equipped with a full array of qualities, we, your audience, would run out of interest in you very quickly. And we probably wouldn't be very polite about it, either!

The point is, you have the qualities to be a great speaker, and no one has more of what it takes than you do. And the more you develop and use your inherent qualities, the richer your speeches, of course, because the richer *you,* the speaker.

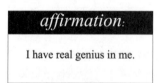

affirmation:

I have real genius in me.

THE QUALIFICATION OF A GREAT SPEAKER

Did you notice that I used the word "qualification" above in the singular—implying that there is only one qualification that one must meet? I did that on purpose.

How does one qualify to become a great speaker? Sometimes it looks like nobody ever does qualify, that nobody can. The standards are too high, too exclusive. You don't qualify because of your height, or your weight, or your race or gender. Or you have certain imperfections or inadequacies that are, well, not acceptable. Or your background isn't right. And your schooling is insufficient. And your psychological problems are too many. And your age, well, your age, all by itself, disqualifies you! Nobody measures up to the impossible standards set by unreasonable, unloving, nudniks who don't measure up to them either. We all fall short of absolutely impossible standards, which are hardly "standard" at all!

Happily, those standards are not worth measuring up to. There is no value, no help, no comfort in words coming from a fixed, sterilized mindset that is without empathy. We are each and all of us modest men and women on this planet—each unique and complete, it is true—but we are also the guy or gal next door, the person you bump into at the market looking for a ripe avocado, the citizen dreading the once again approaching tax time, a proud member of a family whose youngest is graduating high school this spring. None of us are big shots.

I heard Carol Burnet being interviewed one time. The interviewer asked her, "When did you know that you'd made it?" She said, "Made it?! I haven't made it. If I thought I'd made it, I'd be finished!"

We are each and all modest but magnificent journeyers, special in our very modesty. Because it is the quality of modesty that equips us to love. And it is the ability to love that qualifies us to speak. Put another way, you've got to be you. Put to music, "I've got to be me!" That's all. And to the degree that you are, you will have something unique and interesting to say to the rest of us. Honor yourself. And honor your contribution as equal to that of anyone else. I learned this from Nicole Kidman .

Enter Nicole Kidman

I had a dream. Nicole Kidman was in it. We were both scheduled to sing. Nicole Kidman sang first. She was glorious! She had a gorgeous voice and knew exactly how to use it. Everybody loved it. Then it was my turn. I was a nervous wreck. I gave it a shot. I sucked. Couldn't sing to save my soul. Everybody felt sorry for me. Everybody thought I was a dope. I felt terrible.

I woke up. I sat up in my bed in the dark, alone. Poor me. Poor poor me, I thought. Nicole was so good and I was so terrible. How unfair. Then it hit me. "My God, Kathryn! This was *your* dream! *You* were dreaming it and you empowered another person—in *your* dream, *your* world—to sing better than you could, and completely disempowered yourself?!"

I got it. I forgave Nicole Kidman (even though she'd taken Keith Urban off the market) and I thanked our common Source that each of us, every one of us, is uniquely and wonderfully talented. Did I really learn this from Nicole Kidman? Of course, not. That's the point. We get everything directly from our Source. That's why we are all equally, though uniquely, endowed.

My friend Diana, whom I'd coached a few days before her "mother of the bride" speech was due to be given, called me in a mini-panic from an alcove off the wedding reception banquet hall the day of. The father of the groom had just delivered his toast. He was big and loud and dynamic and got a big round of applause. Now Diana, more gentle and soft-spoken, had to follow him. The waiters were just re-filling the champagne flutes! She was reaching out to me for an emergency pep talk!

Fortunately, an image came to my mind—a piano keyboard. "We're all keys on a key-board," I told her. "Some A, some D, some B-flat. But we're all equally beautiful and valuable; we're all *music*. Just be yourself, mean what you're saying, and love them." Diana told me later that this did the trick for her and she was a success.

We are all equal in the "value" department, in "the great piano in the sky." Which is good to know in case you ever have to follow Robin Williams! We each show up on this planet complete and self-sufficient, like a fully loaded Buick on a showroom floor.

"THE ART OF EXTEMPORE SPEAKING"

One of my favorite books on public speaking is called, *"The Art of Extempore Speaking."* It was written by M. Bautain, Vicar-General and Professor at The Sorbonne, at the beginning of the twentieth century, and published in 1915. It is so inspiring and such a joy to read! It is my pleasure to introduce and recommend it to you. You can still find copies of it in on-line bookstores.

Focusing on the eloquence of extemporaneous and, to some degree, impromptu speaking, Bautain advocates trusting "the marriage of one's mind to the moment" to develop the speech. He encourages the speaker to expect and to depend upon the fruitage of his devotion to the truth in his speech.

Bautain developed his own list of abilities and attributes that he thought every great speaker must have. Here are his top seven:

1. A lively sensibility.
2. A penetrating intelligence.
3. A sound reason/good sense.
4. A prompt imagination.
5. A firm, decisive will.
6. A necessity to communicate.
7. A native instinct and talent to speak.

Let's look a little more deeply at these for a moment. I see them like this:

1. <u>A lively sensibility.</u> The desire, the joy, the impulse. The willingness—the urge, in fact—to engage.
2. <u>A penetrating intelligence.</u> Thinking that doesn't take things just on the surface, but actually goes in further to uncover deeper truth. (This is consistent and akin to acting "research" work.)
3. <u>A sound reason/good sense.</u> High intelligence, yes, but also good old common sense. Street smarts. Reason, wisdom; the facts.
4. <u>A prompt imagination.</u> The ability, right in the moment, to be able to step up to the challenge or require-

ment at hand. The ability to roll with the punches without judgment.

5. <u>A firm, decisive will.</u> No double-minded wishy-washiness. Authoritative, and comfortable being so. A quick study with powerful trust in oneself. (So much of this work has to do with self-trust, self-confidence, and self-appreciation!)

6. <u>A necessity to communicate.</u> More than just an urge to engage and communicate, but the actual need to do so. This has to do with "the calling" to speak, the desire to honor truth, and express it.

7. <u>A native instinct and talent to speak.</u> It comes naturally. It is part of who the speaker is. (I agree with M. Bautain that this is necessary to the speaker, but I'm not sure he would agree with my view that this instinct-and-talent is a possession, by birthright, of everyone!)

According to Bautain, it is these abilities and attributes that combine to equip the speaker to deliver a dynamic presentation.

DOING IT FOR YOU!

John Lennon was asked if he wrote his songs for himself or for other people. He said he wrote them for himself. He figured that since he was a product of his time, if he were true to, and wrote for, himself, he would be true to and writing for the other people of his time as well.

I tell my acting students, make sure that your performance is for yourself. You don't do it for an audience; you do it for yourself—your way, the way that you think it should be performed. And the audience will benefit by your authenticity and fidelity. You want to leave the stage, I tell them, with the satisfaction of knowing that you portrayed your character the way you thought he should have been portrayed; that you made the choices that you thought were appropriate; and that you, when in character, meant what you said and said it the way that you meant it—not to please the director, or the audience, or your scene partners—but to please yourself. That much the actor can control and promise and deliver. If you, the speaker, will do that much, in your own voice in your speeches, the integrity of "the one in relation to the whole" is such that others will benefit by your doing so as well.

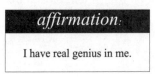

affirmation:

I have real genius in me.

VOICE

What I am about to say now is more common knowledge in the world of writing, but it is true in that of speaking as well. Whether it's on the page or it's being spoken out loud, one of things—one of the main things—editors and readers and audience members are looking for is *a voice*. They, we, want you to sound like somebody. We don't care so much about facts and figures, or good grey reporting; we want to listen to someone who has an attitude.

Voice takes in style, but it's more than style. Voice is what the reader or audience member hears in his mind's ear when the speaker is speaking. It's what gives us the sense that the words are coming from another living human being with a unique perspective. It's not only that we're hearing a story or a speech, but that somebody is *telling it* to us, somebody is *speaking* it. Somebody distinctive that we could pick out of a crowd. Somebody whose voice we'll listen to, and listen *for*, and recognize the next time we hear it. Somebody we can trust.

That's why you've got to ask, in the beginning, when you are first working on your speech, "Who am I?" And all the questions that go with that. "Why am I writing this? What do I believe in? Who am I talking to? What is my objective?" Because in the end, your presentation will sink or swim based on whatever that special thing that you have *is*.

Your *voice* is your sincerity, your integrity and your trust-worthiness. It is your voice put into *character*. It is a rebuttal to the declaration of the misunderstanding salesperson, "I'm always acting (pretending)." *In fact*, the good salesperson is never pretending. He is sincerely extolling the virtues of a product he is proud to be offering his customers. If that isn't true, he has some "aligning" to do. If you believe in what you are doing and saying, you don't have to pretend, or turn your enthusiasm, or your pitch, on and off.

ACTING TIP:
SPEAKING IS AN HONOR; CHERISH IT!

A FEW WORDS ON POWER

Power. That feeling inside that *you matter*. That you make a difference. That what you are doing is not only worthwhile but crucial. You speak with conviction because you are convinced. You speak with authority because you have dominion. You speak with strength because you are developing mastery.

What is it that gives you that glorious sense of power? Ultimately, it's the right motives. The right motives *plug you in*. They right motives illuminate your way and keep you on path. They dissolve confusion and free up your tongue. If your motivation in your speaking is to give, then, somehow, you automatically become plugged in to the providential power source of progress.

At the same time you feel this wonderful psychic power surge, you also realize—and you don't mind this because it makes you feel grounded—that you are a steward to the ideas you are expounding. You are in service to them, a humble and willing medium for the truths that are coming through you to your audience. And this combined humble power feels great! This is the "sweet spot" in speaking. You are a man or woman at work—being, giving, serving—witnessing the entire dance without struggle. This is fun! And you walk off the podium knowing that you have made an impact in the universe this day.

SUMMARY OF MAIN POINTS

1. "Character determines plot." The very words you speak tell us who you are because your nature has determined what you have to say.
2. Decide "who you are"—as character. Define your objectives and goals as a speaker.
3. Consider and imbibe the qualities (and meet the qualification) of a good speaker.
4. You never "finally make it" because the journey doesn't end. You may claim joy and satisfaction at any point along the way at any time, however.
5. You are enough.
6. Never believe that anyone is better—in any way—than you are.
7. Do it for *you*! Do it your way, and the audience will benefit from your originality and authenticity.
8. People are searching for "a voice." We want you to sound like someone, someone specific, with an attitude, somebody we can trust.
9. You are a steward for the ideas you are expounding.

"Here, then, would be an effective guide for the speech-writer, the speaker, and the listener: Write from the heart, deliver from your life, and listen with discernment."

— James S. Rosebush

OUR CHOICES OF TOPICS ARE ENDLESS

Have you ever thought about the fact that there are, literally, thousands of things that you know? From how to tie your shoe laces, to how to use a can opener, to how to lick an envelope in a way that won't cut your tongue? *Thousands*! From the minor, like how to tear off a paper towel so that it doesn't leave a ripped corner remaining, to the more important, like "Watch the cars, not the lights!" which one kind, if gruff, cab driver yelled at me when I first moved to New York. Don't pat the soil down too tightly when you transplant a lily. If you order your fries without salt at a fast food joint they'll have to make them fresh. (And then you can add your own salt!) If you pick at it—a scab, *a relationship*—you'll only aggravate it! Thousands, from the various worlds within our world—of finance, gardening, cooking. How to make the letter "a," small and big. All the things you can do on your computer. The fact that you should never leave the house with a candle burning, and that you should never say anything bad about somebody unless you plan on it eventually getting back to that person. How to apply just the right amount of pressure in a handshake, and how to avoid an accident when you are applying mascara while you are driving!

And these are just some of the things that you know *how to do*. What about the thousands of things you simply *know*? Such as, Pluto was once a planet but now, all of a sudden, it's not! Which is not fair, and opens up a whole can full of worms. (Which you also know how to do!) The thousands of facts! How Christmas is related to the winter solstice, and that yellow mixed with blue makes green, and that it's never too late for a fresh start. It's mind-boggling, isn't it? Or, just the reverse—mind-freeing, mind-inspiring! I mean, congratulations! You are one very smart cookie—because you also know how the things that you know relate to one another, and fit into the bigger picture, and . . . In short, we know lots of stuff, which gives us a very wide array of choices as far as what to talk about goes. It's not like "there's nothing on TV." Because everything that you know, every fact and every experience or memory you have had and possess can be developed into a topic for a speech.

ACTING TIP: BE STILL AND LISTEN.

CHOOSING OUR TOPICS

How do we choose what to speak about, if it is, in fact, within our power to decide? Because, in many cases it's not. We are instructed by our employers or clients to speak on certain business topics; or to give a factual—perhaps, a zoning—report; or, simply, to transfer information. But even within those seemingly done-deal presentations there is always at least some room for creativity. Maybe even a little levity, even a little love. And, like an actor performing a scene, a speaker will call upon her experience and under-standing to bring the speech to life. But using freedom as our template—to the degree that we are "free" to—how do we choose what to speak about?

As noted earlier, what we truly have to say stems natu-rally from who we genuinely are. When we are at our most authentic, our most essential messages flow most effortlessly from our hearts. And the clearer you are about what you have to say, the more abundant the chances that you'll get to say it, because the more likely you will recognize the opportunities "to speak" when they present themselves to you.

THE COSMIC BULLHORN

We all have certain messages that are dear to us and we feel we would like to share. Sometimes, though, to beginning speakers they seem buried or, at best, vague. In my acting workshops I use an exercise to unearth them. It goes like this:

EXERCISE:

"The Cosmic Bullhorn." If I were going to give you the great planetary bullhorn for five minutes, and everybody on the planet was going to stop whatever he or she was doing and listen to you, what would you say? What message would you give to the world?

OK, let's play. I pose that question to you. What would you say to the world?

_____

_____

_____

_____

_____

_____

How did you do? If you are still staring at the blank lines above, that's OK. People's eyes often glaze over at first when I give them this exercise. At first they wonder, should they use the moment as a PR opportunity? "Cast me in your movie!" "Everybody go buy my record!" But when they think about it more deeply, and see it as an opportunity to give something huge to the world, their eyes light up.

affirmation:
I am a life expert. I have the ability to determine what is important to impart to an audience, and to do so effectively.

So let's go again. If we gave you the bullhorn or microphone—if we gave you every computer screen in the world—and for five minutes we were going to listen exclusively to you, what would you tell us?

_____

_____

_____

_____

_____

_____

Good. Now review your answer. This is at least part of "your message," and part of who you are as a person, an artist, a presenter. Remember, the more clear you are about who you are, the more "who you are" and "what you have to say" will align—as well as constitute the content of your presentations.

SOME EXAMPLES, PLEASE

What are some examples of important things that people have to say, messages that speakers—perhaps you—might find worthy to talk about? Eat more chocolate! Have more fun! Very worthy messages, if you ask me. But are they *your* messages?

In his wonderful book, *All I Really Need to Know I Learned in Kindergarten*, Robert Fulghram not only steps up to the plate on this issue, he hits the ball out of the park! His message is a collection of lessons that he learned when he was a young boy, as well as the proposition that they have been enough to sustain him through adulthood. Some of them are:

1. Play fair.
2. Don't hit people.
3. Put things back where you found them
4. Clean up your own mess.
5. Don't take things that aren't yours.
6. Say you're sorry when you hurt somebody.
7. And take a nap every afternoon.

Great, isn't it? His message, as a collection, is terrific. But any one of his lessons could stand alone as a worthy enough message to promote.

OTHER TOPIC IDEAS

Here are some other ideas to prime the pump of your own collection of things that you know, and believe in, and could speak on:

1. Don't look back.
2. Don't doubt or second guess yourself.
3. It's never too late.
4. Happiness is in enjoying the journey.
5. Don't tolerate bullying, from anyone.
6. Life is good.
7. We have dominion over evil. Let's exercise it!
8. There's always a way.
9. Savor the moment.
10. Hope triumphs over experience.
11. Don't believe everything you think!
12. And, of course, have more fun! *(And eat more chocolate!)*

Maybe you want to speak about being kinder to animals, or having more respect for the intelligence of children, or speak against oppression or the notion of male domination. Maybe you wish to stand up and speak out for excellence, expounding the old adage that "anything worth doing is worth doing well," or that "knowledge and spiritual service are only meaningful when they are reflected in action." Perhaps, you want to speak about financial security, or landscape design, or how to diet effectively. You might take a look at The Learning Annex's catalogue for the many classes that they offer. How many of those topics might you be able to speak on? Let alone the many topics or messages that pertain to your particular business—such as new modes of manufacturing, or marketing strategies; or scholastic subjects if you are a teacher; or how to structure political speeches or legal summations.

You can see that the possibilities are endless! *Not for you, though.* They're not. Abundant but not endless. Which is not to limit you in any way. For you, we want the perfect fit—a speech that is unique to you and employs your knowledge and talents and expertise. A speech that lights you up from the inside and makes us glad that we've come to hear you speak!

Your Speaking Topics

Now that you have had a chance to consider some of the above ideas as potential topic suggestions—to, at least, let them prime the pump for you—let's make some choices, at least some temporary ones, to get you in the game.

EXERCISE:

"Five Topics." Write down five topics that you would like to speak about. The resource that is your knowledge, though custom tailored, is still remarkably and beautifully vast! You will never need to worry that you won't have anything to say! Say it now, in fact, won't you?

1. _____

2. _____

3. _____

4. _____

5. _____

HALLOWEEN PERSONAS AND FIVE DREAM LIVES

Good! Keep that on hand. Now here is another exercise—a two-parter—that will give you even more ideas to speak about. These are fun!

EXERCISE:

"Personas and Dream Lives."

- Five Halloween Personas. List the five most fun "characters" you dressed up as (or were dressed up by others as) for Halloween. (For me, this included dressing as a princess, a queen—I was big on having power—and a ballerina. So, three for me. How about five for you?) If you can't make five, supplement your list with characters you would like to have gone as.

1. _____

2. _____

3. _____

4. _____

5. _____

- <u>Five Dream Lives</u>. This one is especially fun. Here goes. Say you have five lives. List the five careers (one per life) you would choose to practice *if you were 100% guaranteed that you would be 100% successful in them.* No side effects. You're not going to go to hell or lose your family. No punishment for success! All good!

1. _____

2. _____

3. _____

4. _____

5. _____

Now analyze your answers. Does this give you further ideas for topics to speak about?

HOW MANY IDEAS PER CUSTOMER?

In the film, *Rebecca*, adapted by Alfred Hitchcock from the novel written by Daphne du Maurier, the lead character, played by Joan Fontaine, speaks about her father, an artist, who spent his whole life painting the same tree over and over again. She makes the point that sometimes artists stay with one subject, one idea, one topic throughout their entire careers. That's their cosmic assignment, as they see it—to explore deeply and exclusively one idea.

For some people, that works. The theatrical actor who has been doing the same part on Broadway eight shows a week for the past fifteen years comes to mind, for instance. Others want something new to explore and express each moment. They want to do Shakespeare in the Park, have a television series, do commercials, do volunteer work at their local YMCA, and give Adult Ed classes in high-profile dating. All at once!

I say, do as many and as much as you want to. ("You are the boss of your life!") But whether you find it more fulfilling to speak on one topic or on many, you, the speaker, like every actor does, have a natural niche. And part of the fun of launching into the world of public speaking lies in discovering what that is.

> **ACTING TIP:**
> PARTICULARIZE AND PERSONALIZE
> TO MAKE YOUR SPEECH RELEVANT.

MY MAIN ROLE AS YOUR COACH

I'm happy to have been able to give you some suggestions as to subject matter. But no matter what the nature of your content is, or the quantity of topics that constitutes it, let me remind you that my main role in your efforts is to help you successfully *perform* whatever that content shall be. Whether you are going to be performing the big speeches, or you are going to be giving business speeches and pitches or presentations, or you'll be teaching or lecturing, or if you will be making one of the smaller speeches—which we do every day in the form of introductions and announcements and toasts—in all of them you will be using virtually the same skills. And it is going to be my pleasure to help you claim and develop those skills to the end that you will be telling your truth with greater confidence and fearlessness.

> **affirmation:**
> I know that every member of my audience will benefit from my presentation.

Take comfort. You don't have to get out there and perform until you are thoroughly prepared and ready to do so. But you have to *get* ready. And—if this isn't obvious—by the time you perform you have to *be* ready!

SUMMARY OF MAIN POINTS

1. Your choices for topics to speak on are endless. But they're not all *your* topics.
2. The clearer you are about who you are, the clearer you will be about what you have to say, and the greater the chances are that you will say it because the more likely you'll recognize and take the opportunities to do so.
3. Become very familiar with your topics.
4. Speak on as many topics as you like, but recognize that every speaker has a niche unique and most natural to him. Part of the fun of launching into speaking is discovering what that is.

PART TWO

The Techniques

CHAPTER FOUR

How to Use This Book—An Overview

"My system will never manufacture inspiration. It can only prepare a favorable ground for it."

    —An Actor Prepares by Konstantin Stanislavski

And here we go! This is going to be the fun part, learning and mastering acting techniques used by professional actors all over the world for over one hundred years to help them prepare and perform—ever since Konstantin Stanislavski made his remarkable contribution to theatre in the form of the guiding principle that "Acting is living on stage." These techniques will not only help to open you up to a deeper emotional experience as a speaker, but it will help you feel more in control when you are on stage.

HOW THE TECHNIQUES WERE SELECTED

I selected the acting techniques that I have chosen to explore in this book from those taught to me by teachers and coaches I studied with, from those taught by master teachers whose writings I've read, from those utilized and touted by other actors, and from techniques that I have developed myself while teaching and working with actors over the last twenty-two years. They work. They don't all work for everyone all the time, but they all work often enough for most actors, and now speakers, for me to feel that they are worthy of being included in every speaker's bag of tricks. Or should I say "tool kit?" Because they are not tricks; these techniques are founded on universal truths. That's what makes them so effective. There-fore, you will find that, as an added benefit, these techniques will also be of help to you in other areas of your life.

┌─────────────────────────────┐
│ ▉ *affirmation:* ▉   │
├─────────────────────────────┤
│   It's all working together!│
└─────────────────────────────┘

TAKE THE FORMALITY . . . INFORMALLY

Formally, according to our Table of Contents, we will be working with a certain number of different well-defined techniques. But don't let this structure—even the techniques themselves—become too rigidly defined in your mind. As you will discover, they cross-talk, they combine, and there are exceptions to "the rules." These techniques exist solely to serve you, as the police commissioner the mayor, *at your pleasure.* In a nutshell, along with the exercises and tips and affirmations that accompany them, I present to you herein what I hope you will come to agree is a handy group of techniques that will enrich the whole experience of public speaking for you.

THE EIGHT SECTIONS OF TECHNIQUES

I have assembled the techniques into eight sections, covering the journey of "the speech."

In the first section, Chapter Five, "Techniques For Finding Your Niche 'In The Play'," we explore the idea of the right fit between you, as speaker, and "the roles" you "play," the importance that *you* be the one who makes that determination, your commitment to taking on the role, or speech, and to doing all that it will take for you to master it.

The second section, Chapter Six, is devoted to the first phase of an actor's—and speaker's—preparation: research. It is called, "Techniques For Researching 'The Role'." These techniques deal with the importance of thorough research as a grounding device when creating and substantiating your message. They deal with the need to determine what the heart and soul of your message is, to clarifying and aligning your objectives for delivering that message, to knowing what you want to say so well that you could put it in entirely different words, and to knowing the results that you want your message to achieve.

The next (third) section, Chapter Seven, "Techniques For Learning and Rehearsing 'The Role'," addresses the rehearsal aspect of preparation, including knowing what you are up against and what you are fighting for, rehearsal opportunities, how to "cold-read," how to memorize, how to improvise, as well as the inescapable need to practice!

The next three sections, Chapters Eight, Nine and Ten, deal with the final elements of preparation. Chapter Eight, "Techniques For Relaxing And Warming Up," describes how important it is to relax and warm up physically, vocally and mentally before every performance and lays out the exercises with which to do so. "Chapter Nine, "In the Wings, Nearly Ready!" outlines the components of a successful performance, then encourages the speaker before "take-off"! And Chapter Ten, "How to Handle Stage Fright," addresses, head-on, how to confront and master your biggest foe along the way.

Next comes the main event, section seven: Chapter Eleven, "*It's Showtime! #1:* Performance Techniques That Establish Your Authority," and Chapter Twelve, "*It's Show-time! #2:* Performance Techniques That Connect You With Your Audience." Performance! The scary part! No, not so much at all, *if*. . . if you have done your prep! In this section I discuss dressing for "the part," controlling your body language, your relationship with your audience, how to claim the stage as your own, maintaining credibility, and listening!

And finally, in the eighth section, Chapter Thirteen, "When *Not* To Speak," and Chapter Fourteen, "After 'The End'," I address when not to speak, using humor, "leaving them wanting more," the issues of assessing your performance and following up, what to do between speaking engagements, how to stay performance-ready, and remembering the nobility of your purpose.

Booking the speech, preparing for it, giving it, following up on it, then getting yourself ready for the next one—whether your speech is a long address or a short announcement—this is the speaker's journey.

STANISLAVSKI'S GREAT CONTRIBUTION (AND STRASBERG'S)

Until the turn of the twentieth century, the main mode, or method, of acting was what, today, we call "indicating."

If it was your task as an actor to feel fear at a certain time, you might put your hands up and open your eyes and mouth wide to "indicate" that your character was afraid. You didn't really feel fear; you just indicated that you felt it. When Konstantin Stanislavski came from Russia to New York with his Moscow Art Theatre in 1922, things changed. He said, in essence, "Out with this indicating nonsense; let's really feel the feelings." And he came up with his famous statement that changed drama forever, "Acting is living on stage." But how can an actor do that? He can *indicate* all day long, no problem. But how can he, *reliably*, live his character's real feelings on stage every moment in every performance? Well, he can't. When his concentration or energy lags, then—as they will from time to time—what can he do to keep *life* in his performance?

Stanislavski was one of the first to come up with "Techniques" to help the actor. Help him what? Help him to concentrate, help him to imagine, help him to feel confident, teach him to improvise should he forget his lines, help him to relax, to handle fear, to speak his lines with authority—help him achieve for himself, and for his audience, an authentic emotional experience. And his techniques did help his actors, and they revolutionized the presentation of drama throughout the world! He called his body of teachings and techniques, "Stanislavski's System."

Lee Strasberg saw The Moscow Art Theatre perform in New York City and was blown away. Later, when he founded the Group Theatre with Harold Clurman and Cheryl Crawford, he developed his own version of "Stanislavski's System" and called his way of acting "The Method." Method of what? Of making the experience of acting "real" for the actor by using certain techniques. Again, the wonderful news for you, the speaker, is that many of these techniques are just as useful to the public speaker as they are to the actor. After all, you don't want to get up on stage or at the podium and feel unfocused, or nervous, or uninspired any more than an actor does. You want to feel your feelings, mean your statements, and express your ideas with an energy that makes the room crackle with passion, just like an actor does. *That's* why the techniques were developed.

ACTING TIP:
RULE OF THUMB—BE YOURSELF IN
"THE ROLE" AS MUCH AS POSSIBLE.

THE METHOD FOR THE SPEAKER, NOT THE SPEAKER FOR THE METHOD

However . . . and this is a big one! These techniques, as good and useful as they are—are *for the speaker*; the speaker is not for the techniques. The techniques are tools, not rules. They are aids. If they help you achieve a powerful, truthful speaking experience, terrific. If not, "*Out!*"

The same principle applies with regards to your teachers. Hopefully, you will have many teachers and coaches in your life, of all kinds; and you will be nice to us all, pay us on time, and speak kindly about us at parties. But that's all you owe us. Our roles in your life, and the techniques we teach you, are to be of service to you. Never you to us, or to them.

ACTING TIP:
TRUST YOURSELF AND YOUR JUDGMENT
MORE THAN YOU TRUST ANYONE ELSE'S.

DEVELOPING YOUR OWN "METHOD"

I saw Meryl Streep being interviewed by James Lipton on "*Inside the Actor's Studio.*" She was asked how she prepares for a role. She said that the first thing she does is panic; she thinks there's no way she's ever going to be able to do it! Then she turns to page one of the script, and begins. That's the thrill of taking a wild tiger by the tail—overcoming the sense of impossibility. You grow by that. Not only do you meet the task at hand—of creating and performing a great speech—you grow in your confidence that, from now on, you'll be able to deal with whatever life hands you.

Sissy Spacek was interviewed on that same series. She was asked what she wanted from a director. She said, with a smile but you knew she meant business, "Just don't' mess with my process." She had "developed her process." Streep had too, if a less structured one. This is what we all shoot for. We use the help we need, when we can get it; but with practice we grow to depend upon our own minds and expertise, and a method begins to evolve that is *our* method.

HOW TO USE THIS BOOK

Although this book is filled with defined techniques, and facts, and instruction, it is not a textbook. It is more a book of ideas, and suggestions. It is not so much to teach you, as to aid you in implementing more effectively what you really already know.

To that end, all you need to do is read this book with an open mind, consider the ideas philosophically as well as practically, do the exercises that appeal to you, incorporate what makes sense to you, refrain from taking any of it too seriously, and enjoy the process! That's how to use this book.

---

affirmation:

I have my own individual way,
which is intelligently ordered
and directed.

SUMMARY OF MAIN POINTS

1. The acting techniques included in this book were selected from those taught by a variety of master acting teachers as well as from those I have developed myself.
2. Only use what works for you, in your way. But do try the techniques.
3. The techniques are broken down into eight sections, covering the main areas of *finding your niche, research, rehearsal, performance,* and *after the end.*
4. As Stanislavski and other teachers revolutionized acting through the discovery and application of certain techniques that make acting come alive on stage, these techniques offer the same benefits to the many different kinds of public speaking.
5. Try (at least, consider) everything everyone else has to offer you but, eventually, you must develop your own method of working.

CHAPTER FIVE

Techniques for Finding Your Niche "In the Play"

"You must believe with all your heart that what you have to say
to your audience can and will make a difference in their lives."

—Barbara De Angelis, Ph.D.

Technique #1:

FINDING AND EMBRACING YOUR NICHE

I heard a story about Walter Matthau and one of the
producers of the film version of *The Odd Couple*. They were
having lunch in a Beverly Hills restaurant. The producer offered Matthau the part of Oscar, the caustic, messy sports
writer. Matthau said he'd be more interested in playing Felix,
the compulsive-obsessive neurotic, played in the end by Jack
Lemmon, because the character of Felix was off-type for him,
different from what he'd played in the past, more of a challenge. The producer said, "I'm not here to under-write your
creative experiments, Walter. Would you like to play Oscar, or
not?" Matthau may have been creatively adventurous but he
was no fool; he took the part, the one a consensus would agree
he was best suited for, and a terrific film was the result.

YOUR PART "IN THE PLAY"

For an actor, his part "in the play" has two aspects. The
first is his part in society's inter-play—his career, which is to
be an actor. The second is the determination of the types of
roles he is best suited to play in dramatic productions.

Each of us has his niche in life; none of us gets to do
everything. And that's OK—we've got other people to do the
other stuff. The actor who is a good business person knows

that she and her services constitute a product. She may enjoy doing Shakespeare in the park on her own time; but if she hopes to make a living, she knows her product has to match up with and meet a commercial demand. She will do well to discover and trod happily down her own particular path of least resistance, offering her services to play roles she is most likely to be recognized as "right for," in which—because they are the most natural to her—she is also most likely to be cast. This is an actress who *will work*.

> **ACTING TIP:**
> ASK YOURSELF,
> "WHAT AM I FIGHTING FOR?"

TYPE-CASTING IS A GOOD THING

This doesn't limit the actor. There is order and intelligence to the world; there is common sense and appropriateness. There is also the freedom to go outside the box. But that only works if it is intelligent. One can't be kooky just for kookiness' sake after the age of thirteen and expect that to get him anywhere. Instead of an actor asking him- or herself what part will be the most challenging or fun to play, he might ask, "In what role can I best serve the play?" and, consequently, the audience, and, consequently, society?! (And, consequently, himself, because it will cause him *to work* regularly!) "Where can I best be of service?"

KNOW YOUR "PRODUCT"

Therefore, an actor must know his product. If he shows up at the door with an egg beater when his customer is in the market for an orange juice squeezer he is not likely to make the sale. And if he says "my egg beater can also be an orange juice squeezer"—which actors do all the time—his customer is going to lose faith in his concern for her needs and she won't want to do business with him in the future.

FINDING YOUR NICHE AS A SPEAKER

After spending some time considering your persona and place, as discussed in Chapter Three, what has begun to emerge, if it has? What have you determined? Who are you in the arena of public speaking? Are you the speaker of a big speech—an address, for instance? Or a legal summation? Are you the speaker of a smaller speech—an announcement or introduction? Are you the keynote speaker at a convention? Fine. Then you are "the keynote speaker" who is going to open (or close) the convention. Good. Now you have your character. Now you have defined the persona who will *speak*. Are you a spokesperson for a new line of cosmetics? Are you the workshop leader of a course on repairing Tibetan masks? Are you an "expert" member of a panel on writing more effective grant proposals? Each one is good. But define who you are.

How do you do that, though, if you're not clear about it? How do you define yourself as a speaker?

Paul Newman spoke about that. He said that when he started acting he didn't think he was very good at it; he didn't think he had the knack as many others had. He couldn't honestly define himself as an actor. But he really wanted to, so he worked very hard to become the actor he wanted to be. And he did it. He developed himself into it. And he didn't try to sell "his product" until he had become it. And by the end of his career he was quite happy with what he had created. This proves to me that much can be cultivated from desire.

affirmation:

I have my own individual way, which is intelligently ordered and directed.

DETERMINING YOUR DESIRE

Where does your *desire* as a speaker lie? What would you *like* to talk about? Would you like to work for a corporation and travel from sales office to sales office throughout the country, motivating the company's sales staff? Would you like to be a preacher and share the good news in a small country chapel, or in football stadiums across the world? Would you like to speak on behalf of the board of directors at your club's annual meetings? Would you like to run for an elected position on your city's school board? Determining your desire as a speaker constitutes the backbone of all your efforts in that arena, if you honor and follow it. If authentic, it constitutes your purpose. Here's an exercise that will help you define where you are at this moment.

EXERCISE:

"Cocktail Party Spiel" (In two parts, two parts each.)

PART ONE:

1a) Pretend that you are at a lavish (Is it Hollywood? Is it The Hamptons?) cocktail party. You have your crystal champagne flute in hand. Here comes your host or a star you've always wanted to meet. Introductions. Then he asks you the question: "What do you do?" Write down your *honest* answer.

_____

_____

_____

_____

_____

_____

1b) If you are not satisfied with your honest answer, write down what you would like to be true.

_____

_____

_____

_____

_____

_____

Part Two (similar but, oh, so different):

2a) Pretend that you are at an *un*-lavish (Is it a back alley? Is it under some bridge?) cocktail party. You have your paper cup of warm beer in hand. Here comes the leader of the psycho-pack. No introductions. He asks you, "Who the #$@! are you and what are you doing here?!" Write down your *honest* answer.

_____

_____

_____

_____

_____

_____

2b) If you are not satisfied with your honest answer, write down what you would like to be true.

_____

_____

_____

_____

_____

Analyze your answers! How do you perceive yourself today? How do you wish to be perceived by yourself and by others? From this "place," *what do you have to say?*

Technique #2:

CASTABILITY PROFILING

I have developed for my acting students a process that helps them determine the types of roles they are most suited to play. I call this process "castability profiling." It helps them analyze who they are as actors in the marketplace. In short, it consists of a group of five exercises that gives them insight and guidance into the types of roles that they believe are the most natural for them to play.

CASTABILITY PROFILING FOR ACTORS

It works like this. You might like to try it. If so, play along:
1. I ask them to: List ten actors of the opposite gender whom you like, plus something you like about their acting. And it can't be, "I like Tom Cruise's smile." But if it is Tom Cruise, it might be: "because he keeps a sincere focus even when he is being humorous." Ten actors, ten reasons.

2. Then I ask them to: List ten actors of the same gender whom you like, plus something you like about their acting. And it can't be, "I like Meryl Streep's gown choices at the different award shows she attends." But if Meryl Streep is one of the actors she chooses, it might be: "because she is fiercely passionate underneath her seemingly casual demeanor."

3. Then I say, "Now, assume you are presently a big star, taking the lead roles, making the big bucks. List ten *other* stars working today (besides you) whom a producer or director would also consider (along with you) for a role—should you have to back out at the last minute and he need to replace you, for instance. Then list three roles that you have seen each of these star actors play.

For example: If the actor was a big star, and Martin Scorsese had to replace him as the lead in his next movie because Steven Spielberg was going overtime on the movie the actor was starring in for him, the actor may think that Scorsese would consider replacing him with Robert Downey, Jr., who the actor saw play *a late nineteenth century detective* (In *Sherlock Holmes), a wealthy industrialist activist* (In *Robocop),*and *an out of control collegiate drug addict* (In *Less Than Zero).*

4. Fourth, I ask the actor to: List ten roles you feel you could comfortably play, along with the main action of the character in the situation, and its resolution.

For example: If the actor is a man he might say, "An outlaw. Who finally finds a good reason to go straight and who makes his own call about what's right—even though he will have to pay society's price for it." If the actor is a woman she might say, "A waitress in a small town. Who starts her own business on the side, angering her neighbors who feel she outshines them, until she lifts them up too." You get the picture? Do ten.

What the actor is unearthing for himself or herself from within his or her own psyche through this exercise, is the way

71

he sees himself as an actor in today's marketplace. This also helps him to realize that he, too, can be a player on the field. Plus, it gives him the opportunity to make any adjustments to his self-image that he chooses to make.

5. Finally, I ask the actor to: Analyze all of the above for insights into what you believe is currently your most probable castability. The actor may then, of course, break all the "rules" if he likes, especially once his foot is in the door through finding his niche. But, again, the value of this exercise is that it helps him see that he has a place, and that he is most likely to be cast, to be used, to be included—in that place—among the active acting populace. And that's a great feeling.

CASTABILITY PROFILING FOR PUBLIC SPEAKERS

Can this process help you find your niche as a speaker? Let's find out. Let me help you reveal to yourself your own ideas of where you feel you best fit in the world as a speaker.

EXERCISE:

"Castability Profiling For Public Speakers."
(In three parts.)

PART ONE:

A. List five speeches that you have heard or read that you "liked." For example: Martin Luther King's "I Have A Dream" speech.
B. Note something about each one that moved you in some way. For example: You were moved by its message of the right of freedom for all people.
C. Note something you "liked" about the speaker's presentation of it (if you heard it). For example: You were impressed by Dr. King's passionate commitment to the ideas he was expressing.

(NOTE: "Liked" will most often be an understatement but you must have at least liked it.)

OK? Here we go:

1.   A. Speech (that I liked:) _____

         _____

         _____

         B. Something I found inspiring or that moved me: ___

         _____

         _____

         C. Something I liked about the speaker's presentation:

         _____

         _____

         _____

2.   A. Speech (that I liked:) _____

         _____

         _____

         B. Something I found inspiring or that moved me: ___

         _____

         _____

         C. Something I liked about the speaker's presentation:

         _____

         _____

         _____

3.   A. Speech (that I liked:) _____

_____

_____

B. Something I found inspiring or that moved me: ___

_____

_____

C. Something I liked about the speaker's presentation:

_____

_____

_____

4.   A. Speech (that I liked:) _____

_____

_____

B. Something I found inspiring or that moved me: ___

_____

_____

C. Something I liked about the speaker's presentation:

_____

_____

_____

5.   A. Speech (that I liked:) _____

_____

_____

B. Something I found inspiring or that moved me: ____

_____

_____

C. Something I liked about the speaker's presentation:

_____

_____

_____

Good! That's good work! You are unearthing in yourself your innate standards and preferences as to what you feel constitutes a good speech, as well as a good speaker. You are pulling up, from your own inner files, your own understanding of where you fit as a speaker.

> ### *affirmation:*
> I am in my right place
> every moment.

A NOTE ON JUST BEING YOURSELF!

Do note this, too, won't you: Don't try to impress the rest of us. It won't work. We care about you as a speaker only insofar as you are uniquely yourself. So if, in the above exercise, you wrote down all "important" speeches, when the speeches you've really liked were all given by standup comics such as Steve Martin, Richard Pryor or Woody Allen, then you've missed the mark! Those guys are brilliant! We needn't be embarrassed because we love them! Besides, we're all doing the same work, anyway—comic, activist, minister; we're all working for the Truth. So what we need from *you* is *your* point of view, *your* take on it all—no matter how dorky you are afraid it will seem. So let's not apologize—or homogenize. Let's get better acquainted with "our stuff," and then strut it!

PART TWO:

Imagine that you are one of the world's five biggest star speakers, and, therefore, given free reign to speak on any topic of your choosing to sold-out arenas. In order of importance to you, what five topics do you speak on, why, and what—in ten words or less—is the crux of your message?

1. Topic:_____

_____

_____

I speak on this topic because:_____

_____

_____

My message (in ten words or less) is:_____

_____

_____

_____

2.   Topic:_____

_____

_____

I speak on this topic because:_____

_____

_____

My message (in ten words or less) is:_____

_____

_____

_____

3.   Topic:_____

_____

_____

I speak on this topic because:_____

_____

_____

My message (in ten words or less) is:_____

_____

_____

_____

4.   Topic:_____

_____

_____

I speak on this topic because:_____

_____

_____

My message (in ten words or less) is:_____

_____

_____

_____

5.   Topic:_____

_____

_____

I speak on this topic because:_____

_____

_____

My message (in ten words or less) is:_____

_____

_____

_____

Excellent! Fun, too, right?

PART THREE:

If you were a star speaker engaged to speak on one of your topics above and something came up to prevent you from making the engagement, and the people who hired you (to speak to thousands!) had to hire someone else to pinch hit for you, list three people you think they might consider as appropriate to replace you. (These can be other famous speakers speaking today, a celebrity, or anyone else.) And why do you think they would choose them?

1.   My replacement might be:_____

_____

_____

Because:_____

_____

_____

2.   My replacement might be:_____

_____

_____

Because:_____

_____

_____

3.   My replacement might be:_____

_____

_____

Because:_____

_____

_____

Good again! Now analyze all three parts of the above exercise. Just spend a little time thinking about it. Ideas will come!

Technique #3:

NAMING YOUR ROLE:
THE SPEAKER AS "CHARACTER"

As stated earlier in this chapter, just as a character in a play performance has a name, so, too, should the role or part that the speaker is "playing" be named. Name the "role" you are playing, as well as the role's main action.

"I am *a junior accountant, presenting a report on earnings for the last quarter.*" That is the role you are playing.

"I am *an association member presenting my suggestions for the agenda for our next quarter.*"

"I am *the hostess of a dinner party, keeping the conversation at dinner lively.*"

This helps you as a speaker because it defines and directs your identity and action, it takes the attention off of you and puts it onto your performance, and it helps you to shape your career according to your own design.

Technique #4:

ACCEPTING THE PART AS YOUR OWN

Whether you initiate and write your speech yourself, or are speaking on assignment, it is crucial to the success of your presentation that you commit fully to taking it on and bringing it to a successful delivery. That doesn't mean just going along and thinking, "Uh-huh, it's on the calendar. I should probably start thinking about it." It means—well, you know what it means. It means figuring out how much time you need to put into it to make it rock and then giving it that much time!

THE "YES" FACTOR

The reason to be so firm in actively accepting your assignment is that doing so opens your psyche to the "yes" factor. The supportive influence of the universe comes into play to back us up when we decide (*decide,* not just fool around with it) that we're going to "make" something—a movie, a speech, a bed—and says "count me in!" It's like an "on" switch that says, "This is a go!" When you accept the assignment to present a speech, you are signing up to affect the careers and, perhaps, the lives of many people who will be counting on you. And you are tapping into the universal supportive influence to back you in your efforts.

Technique #5:
ACCEPTING THE NEED TO ASSERT YOURSELF

When I take on new students or clients, I require that they always agree to perform when asked. Opportunities to perform come at unexpected moments and, because they do, one had better be ready. This fact sets us on the path of *becoming* ready.

But what if nobody asks you to perform? People are busy and self-concerned; and to a degree that's how it should be. Consequently, you may find yourself in a conference room where everyone but you has had his say and the meeting is about to break up. What should you do—slink off fuming, or start crying? Or try to convince yourself that it doesn't matter that you didn't have your say? No. None of the above. You need to self-assert. The nature of the circumstances will prompt you as to how. "Excuse me. Before we adjourn there's something I'd like to say, if I may," you might say. Or, "My turn?" Or, "Of course, there is something else worth mentioning." It doesn't have to be rude—there's a difference between *aggressive* and *assertive*. But there is also a big difference between *assertive* and being weak. You will like yourself a whole lot more, for one thing, when you assert yourself. Plus, "we the people" will benefit from your contribution.

> **ACTING TIP:**
> TAKE AN ACTING CLASS.
> *(Really. You'll love it.)*

Acknowledging Yourself as An Authority

Once you have found your niche, and accepted and committed to the part as your own, and have stepped up assertively as you felt it was called for, you are ready to acknowledge yourself as an authority on your topic. You may, in fact, be but "an authority-in-the-making," but take it on—the authorship—and demonstrate it as you go, step by step. Like Paul Newman, prove it by creating and becoming it.

Now comes the heavy lifting—the work of becoming truly performance-ready!

SUMMARY OF MAIN POINTS

1. "Type-casting," especially in the beginning of an actor's or a speaker's career, is a good thing; it helps him get his foot in the door.
2. Know what "your product" (*you*) can do. Define yourself as a commodity.
3. Let your desire point the way for you.
4. "Castability Profiling" is a very effective method by which to discover, define and marshal your marketability as a speaker.
5. Claim and name the part you are playing—The Public Speaker. Doing so helps to direct your action.
6. Accepting your role as "a speaker" opens you up to the" yes" factor, the universal supportive influence that comes into play when we *decide* to create something.
7. Learn to self-assert, and to acknowledge yourself as an authority.

CHAPTER SIX

Techniques for Researching "The Role"

"The first and most important approach for the actor is to read the play and find out what the playwright wants to say to the world."

—Stella Adler

THE THREE CATEGORIES OF PREPARATION

Preparation for an acting role consists of three main categories of activity—research, rehearsal, and relaxation and warm up. The first, the actor does pretty much by herself. The second, she does with her scene partners, and the third—relaxation and warm-up—she does on her own before every rehearsal and performance. Let's talk about the all-important groundwork of research, and how that relates to you, the speaker.

> ### affirmation:
> I delight in being thoroughly
> prepared, and am willing
> to do the work to become so.

RESEARCHING "THE ROLE"—EIGHT STEPS

We are so sophisticated in the world of drama today, aren't we? We've seen so many plays—in the theatre, on television, on-line—and so many actors being interviewed about their work, that, whether we're actors or not, we have a pretty good idea about what it takes to research an acting role. What it comes down to is that the actor works until he gets to the point where, when he is delivering his lines during his performance, we the audience (and more importantly, he himself), believe him. That work consists of several steps.

Step #1: Constructing The Character's Biography. The actor constructs a history of his character that has led him to where we first meet him in the play. This gives the actor empathy and insight into the choices his character made in his past that got him to where he is now, where the actor steps in and takes him over. Unless the actor has belief in and compassion for his character's reality and condition, the audience won't either. And, consequently, we won't learn from his experience.

Step #2: Assigning Substitutions. Say the character was an only child, raised in the mid-west, and had an idealized concept of what it meant to serve in the military. He went off to war, was injured, came back . . . And this is where we meet him in the play. He is now in the hospital, facing the fear that he will never recover. He meets a woman who seems quite enthralled with him, which challenges his dark sense of his condition and . . .

Now, the actor may have come from a family of ten and may never have been to war, nor to the mid-west. But to "play" this character with conviction, he has to "get himself there." How does he do this? He does it by what is known as "assigning substitutions." He substitutes, from his own life, experiences that were as close to those of his character as he can find in his memory, in order to relate to him. He did not go to war but he did have a severe conflict with a colleague, and he was in a street fight one time and got the tar knocked out of him. He has never been to the mid-west but his best friend is from Iowa.

Step #3: Conducting Interviews. Talk to people. Interview the experts as well as others who have a stake in your presentation. (See more in "On Conducting Interviews" later in this chapter.)

Step #4: Reading All About It. In addition to constructing his character's biography and assigning substitutions, an actor may decide to read up in areas where his first-hand experience or knowledge is limited. He may read a history of World War II.

Step #5: "Getting To Know You." The actor has created his character's biographical history but what is his character really *like*? This includes such things as the sports he plays, his cultural interests and politics, his religion—how that might affect his belief that he will, or will not, recover, for instance, his vocal dialect and the way he dresses. The actor adds these features to round out the personality of his character.

Step #6: Knowing What One Is Talking About. "Obviously!" you say? Obviously *not* as much as it should be! But the actor has got to know, and mean, what he, as his character, is saying. And if he is not sure about something—which is all too common—he's got to find out.

Step #7: Reading the Part Aloud Ten Times. When an actor begins to research a role, I advise that she reads the play, in its entirety, ten times. No, I'm not kidding and, yes, I'm aware that ten times is a lot of times. But new information comes to the reader with each reading. We don't stay at the same degree of concentration all the way through each reading. So, in reading number eight the actor might pick something up that she missed in reading number two.

Step #8: Paraphrasing the Part. When an actor can put his part into his own words, using as much or as little of the actual written text as he likes, he can rest assured that he has pretty much got the gist of the piece.

Technique #6:

SPENDING TIME IN THE ALMIGHTY ARMCHAIR

Where does the actor do this and the other components of his research? He does it in what I call "the almighty armchair." I call it "almighty" because worlds—certainly "characters"—are created there. But it can be any kind of chair; and it can be euphemistic—not a chair at all but a state of mind, a state of deep and thorough "research and development" of his character. The actor—or speaker—has got to be willing to spend the time that it takes, in his "armchair."

RESEARCH IS EQUALLY CRUCIAL TO THE SPEAKER

You begin to see how important thorough research is to an actor when working on a part. But can you see the importance of research to good preparation when you are working on a speech? Or legal argument? Or a pitch?

Maybe a salesman is making a sales pitch. That man needs to know everything about his product, its relevance to his customer's needs, and be ready to answer all questions. That knowledge, which he gains from his research—his reading, his conversations with the chemists who created the product, for instance—will under-pin and support his pitch more securely than any bravado he could muster through the idea that he is always "acting." Real confidence based on authentic knowledge—the real thing—never has to be "sold."

DINNER PARTY RESEARCH?

What if you were preparing to host a dinner party? Would the technique of spending some time in your "armchair" in research help you in your preparation? Let's see.

EXERCISE:

"Dinner Party Research." Let's say you plan to host a dinner party and you want it to be the social event of the year. How might doing some research contribute to your success as a host? What comes off the top of your head? List three ways research beforehand might help you in your role of "successful host of a dinner party?"

1. _____

   _____

   _____

2. _____

   _____

   _____

3. _____

   _____

   _____

Did either of the following make your list?

A. Knowing the biographical backgrounds of your guests would help you to discover things that your guests have in common, which could influence the order in which you seat them—together, or maybe, *apart*.

B. Having researched the employment history of your guests, when a topic is discussed on which one of your guests happens to be an expert, you would be able to say, for instance, "Tony, tell us your idea on that one."

Yes! Research is always powerful. It makes all the difference in the world between a successful presentation and a mediocre one. No matter the length of your speech, be ready. Be prepared. And don't say anything that you don't have a clear and honest meaning for.

ACTING TIP:
LOVE DOING THE ARMCHAIR WORK.

Technique #7:
  THE SPEAKER'S SPEECH IS HIS MONOLOGUE

The paper that you hold in your hand—your speech—is to you, the speaker, as a monologue is to an actor. You, too, should read your speech aloud *at least* ten times before you begin your deeper work on it. See what's in it—whether you wrote it or someone else did. What is "your character"—*you*—saying? What point do you wish to make? What is your bottom line?

You Are a Life Expert

The reason you need to know your material so well is that the part you are playing as a public speaker is "an expert in your topic or field." If you plan to give a six minute talk on the parking lot problem at your son's school, you've got to know what you are talking about, not just get through it and hope nobody asks any questions! You've got to know what the problem is, what the laws and regulations are, who's on what side, why you think your idea of how to fix it will work, as well as case histories covering all of these points. *And* you've got to be ready for the opposition that, I guarantee you, is coming your way! But that's part of the fun of it. That's you being up there, being prepared, being an expert, making a difference, *working*—keeping the world going. And growing.

On Conducting Interviews

I recently gave a four-week seminar/workshop for the docents at The Museum of Art and Design in New York City.

It was called, "Presenting . . . *You!* Acting Techniques that Make Presentation and Public Speaking Fun and Fearless." I'm pleased to say it was very successful, one of the reasons for which I attribute to the research/prep tactic of *talking to people*. I got permission from their equivalent of Human Resources to speak to two docents by telephone and I simply chatted with them about my upcoming event. I asked them: Had they ever attended a workshop like mine? What did they like, what didn't they like? What were they expecting from me? What were they hoping I would *not* offer? What would have to happen for them to feel the event had been a success? Then we just visited a bit. When I walked into the meeting room the first day of the seminar and met Carol and Diane face to face for the first time, I felt a sense of warmth and welcome from them. And they knew that I was invested in giving them a rewarding experience.

EXERCISE:

"The Pre-Engagement Interview." Think of a group with whom you might try this tactic of pre-interviewing some of your attendees or audience members. Who might you interview, and what might you ask them? (What would you, in fact, like to know from them ahead of time that might help you make a better presentation?)

I would interview: _____

_____

_____

I would ask:_____

_____

_____

Don't be afraid to solicit ideas and information from other people. You will be the one who decides whether or not to include them in your presentation. Most of the time you will get something good out of it. And don't be afraid to tell stories on yourself—good or bad—if they support your point. Stories and case histories help people "relate."

MUSICALIZE IT!

Make sure you've got the rhythm of the words of your speech in your mouth in a way that both pleases the ear and transports their meaning. As much as the sentiments of the speech will allow, let the words be dispatched by an almost poetic level of delivery. When we are in touch with our emotions, and honest, there's always a sense of music to our expression. Find that musicality. Feel the feelings. Because the words follow the feelings and exist to express them. Can you say what you are saying in a more precise and pleasing way to your own ear? If so, do it. It will enliven your listeners. We the audience want that. We want that passion. That's what keeps us in our seats, *involved.*

Technique #8:
"WHAT IS YOUR SPEECH *ABOUT*?"

It is the most commonly asked question of any artist's or performer's piece of work. *What is it about?* "I'm writing a book." "Really? What is your book about?" "I'm in a movie." "Oh? What is the movie about?" "I'm giving a speech at the U.N. today." "Oh, wow! What about?" The simplest and most often asked question. And the most difficult for the artist or speaker to answer, although it is the most important question that he should ask himself.

DEVELOPING YOUR "LOG LINE"

Knowing what your speech is about, stated in a direct short sentence or two—a log line (sometimes known as the "TV Guide blurb")—will solve both problems. It will answer your clients' inquiry and it will serve *you* as both a guiding light and an anchor in both the preparation and the delivery of your speech.

Spend some time on developing the log line for your speech. Hone it. Edit it until you are pleased with its preciseness. Then you will be able, every few moments during your performance, to silently remind yourself by recalling your log line what your piece is really about, and to continue to allow that engine to drive your delivery.

Technique #9:
CLARIFYING AND ALIGNING YOUR OBJECTIVES

If your "log line" states the story of your speech, the "super-objective" defines the main objective point, or moral, of that story.

DETERMINING THE "SUPER-OBJECTIVE"

When working on a play, the actor needs to know the main point, or "super-objective," of the play as a whole, as well as the main objective of all the characters in the play, including his own. As a speaker, you need to know the super-objective of your speech, as well as the main reasons your audience is desirous of hearing you. Doing the following exercise will show you how to determine those objectives and desires.

EXERCISE:
"Determining Your Super-Objective." (Use this as a template for determining the "super-objective" of any speech.)

1. State the topic of your speech:_____

_____

_____

2. Why are you giving it?_____

_____

_____

3.   What do you want to achieve?_____

_____

_____

_____

4.   Who is your ideal audience?_____

_____

_____

_____

5.   Why do they want to hear your speech?_____

_____

_____

_____

6.   What will have had to happen for you to be able to consider your speech succesful?_____

_____

_____

_____

CHECKING THE "IN SYNC" FACTOR

The exercise above calls to mind "the bigger picture" and the bigger question: What is the "super-objective" of our lives? I don't think this is the place to explore that question in great depth but let's do this much—check in with yourself to see if what you wish to speak about is consistent with your life-goals and values. Let's do that as an exercise.

EXERCISE:

"Checking The *In Sync* Factor. " (In three parts.)

PART ONE: List ten objectives that you have for your life. They can be big ones—"Climb Mt. Hugeness" in whatever form that takes for you; an objective of self-improvement, such as "Learn to play the piano;" or a smaller objective, such as "Clean out the garage."

1. _____

2. _____

3. _____

4. _____

5. _____

6. _____

7. _____

8. _____

9. _____

10. _____

PART TWO: List ten topics that you do, or would like to, speak about. Your topic may have as its matrix one or more of the larger speeches, such as "corporate teamwork" or a political speech on "urban pride;" or you may be a salesperson who wants to successfully sell his new line of office products. Or you may be an attorney, or a business CEO, or an assistant public relations person, or the membership chair at your local Junior Woman's Club. Maybe it's a combo. List ten.

1. _____

2. _____

3. _____

4. _____

5. _____

6. _____

7. _____

8. _____

9. _____

10. _____

PART THREE: Analyze the above two lists. Are they in sync? Are you speaking about what you love and believe, and is relevant to you? Are you "on-purpose" in your life? If not, it's never too late to make adjustments.

Technique #10:
PARAPHRASING YOUR SPEECH

Now that you have your log line (the story) and know the super-objective (the main point) of your speech, the next step you might take in the area of research is to paraphrase your speech.

There are many ways to improvise in the world of public speaking, and we will explore several of them throughout this book, especially in Chapter Seven. For our purposes at this stage of preparation, however, I simply want you to put your speech in your own words. Use as much or as little of the actual written text as you like, but get through the whole speech. You can do this in different posture positions—standing up, lying down, hanging out a window, or speaking your lines through a straw—whatever you like. Just make sure that you are able to cover and express all the main points in your speech in your own—or different—words. If you can do that much, you're in good shape, you've got the drift of your speech.

Notice, we've done no memorization yet, and I don't want you to do any. You're getting a good, strong organic dose of the piece, and there's still more work to be done before you are ready to memorize it. Do this paraphrase improv once or twice, in your armchair, in your bathtub—wherever you like—till you think you could "wing it" if you had to. This is valuable psychic insurance. Then quit. I don't want you to commit inadvertently an imprecise version to memory.

LOVE THE PREP

There was a time in my life when I was living in Hermosa Beach, working with a personal fitness trainer/masseur named Harold. As part of my monthly training package, Harold gave me a massage every two weeks. He was this big handsome African-American sports trainer, and we had lots of fun working out to great rock and roll music three times a week in my backyard a block from the beach. There was some minor flirtation going on between us here and there but when it came time for my massage, the rock and roll would stop, the physical activity would stop, the fooling around would stop, and Harold would become the Big Kahuna, high priest at the altar of his massage table and I would be his client whom he was there solely to serve. His attitude became reverent, he tied his special bandana around his forehead, he did a short meditation, and he remained silent throughout the massage (which was fantastic!).

Harold loved the prep. He took the work he was about to do seriously, and he prepared for it. Once I was back off the table, I had to once again keep an eye on my virtue. (Just kidding. Where are you, Harold, my old friend?) But while I was on the table I knew I was safe. Harold understood that to do a really good job, the job starts in the preparation.

Love the prep. Love the research, rehearsal and warm up—love *all* the prep. *Decide* to. Don't try to rush through it, to get it out of the way so you can get to the *real* work. This *is* the real work—every bit as much as performance is. Take your time with it. Live it, love it.

> **ACTING TIP:**
> ACCEPT EVERY CHALLENGE,
> EVERY OBSTACLE, AS AN OPPORTUNITY.

BUT WHAT IF YOU DON'T LOVE IT?

If, however, you don't want to do this homework, this armchair preparation, then you don't really want to be a speaker. Not really. Not be what a speaker really is and does for society. Not if you don't want to do a really good job for us. You may want the thrill of being on stage, of being in a position of power, which is fine. But you don't really want to pierce veils and move mountains in the hearts of your listeners. Because, as in acting, speaking is like an iceberg. Most of it— the preparation, the hours, the days, the *weeks* of construction and reconstruction—lay beneath the surface. Only the tip— founded upon the prep you did in your armchair and, later, in your rehearsals—appears above the surface in performance.

If you *do* want to speak, however, and are willing to expend the effort, you will find there is nothing stressful in doing this armchair work. What is stressful is *not* doing it, and then getting up there on stage knowing you're not prepared. *That's* stressful! But if you do your prep, when you get up on stage or at the podium nothing can topple you. You will be on a solid foundation. You will *be* a solid foundation. And the joy of speaking will make up for all the work that goes into it and prove more than worth it.

---

affirmation:

I acknowledge and am grateful
that my success is inevitable.

Technique #11:
KNOWING HOW THE PLAY IS MEANT TO END

Some actors will tell you that they feel the most comfortable in their lives when they are on stage. This is not surprising. On stage, actors' lives are completely under control. heir reality is certain. They know how the play is going to unfold and they know how it is meant to end. They know what the other characters are going to say all along the way, and that when it's *their* turn to talk no one is going to interfere with them in any way that is not scripted. There are no surprises on stage—apart from the occasional prop accident or "wardrobe malfunction," or if somebody forgets his lines and you've got to jump in and save the day. But, as a rule, "life" is certain on stage. Life is *known*. This makes the actor feel secure.

It is equally stabilizing and comforting to the public speaker to know how her speech is "meant to end"—to know before you give it how you want it to turn out, the response and results you hope to receive and achieve by your presentation of it. This image of success in your mind will serve as a guiding light to help keep you on track during your performance and to let you know if you are falling aside. You'll want to maintain a sense of flexibility as you go along, of course, but the choices to bend or veer off your path will be made by you, not by chance.

But what gives you the right and the power to expect a successful end? Your confidence lies in the truth of what you are saying and your skill in presenting it well, both of which come from your thorough research and preparation work. You *deserve* to be successful. It isn't magical; it is logical that you will have arrived—you will have prepared for it!

SUMMARY OF MAIN POINTS

1. Acting preparation consists of research, rehearsal, and relaxation and warm up.
2. Researching a role for an actor consists of several steps:
    a. Constructing the character's biography
    b. Assigning substitutions (from his own life)
    c. Reading and interviewing
    d. Getting to know the character—assigning intimate details
    e. Having a meaning for everything you say
    f. Reading your character's words aloud ten (10) times
    g. Paraphrasing the part
3. Research is equally valuable to the speaker.
4. Additional research by the speaker includes:
    h. Interviewing your prospects
    i. Developing your log line
    j. Clarifying and aligning your objectives
    k. Determining your super objective
    l. Paraphrasing your speech
5. Love the prep.
6. Know how "the play" is meant to end.

CHAPTER SEVEN

Techniques for Learning And Rehearsing "The Role"

"After all the imagination and the dreams, it gets down to the job."

— Pierce Brosnan

DEFINING REHEARSAL

Rehearsal includes doing everything you need to do after you have completed your research to make yourself feel that you are ready to step forward and perform your part. Let's look at some of the components and benefits of a good rehearsal.

Technique #12:
MAXIMIZING THE OPPORTUNITIES
EVERY REHEARSAL INCLUDES

There are many opportunities inherent in every intelligent, well-structured rehearsal. Here are six big ones:

1. The opportunity to learn to roll with the punches.

   Rehearsal for an actor includes the preparation and practice work the actor does with others in the play before his actual performances. The actor may think that he knows his material, that he "got it down pat" in his private research and learning work, until he becomes involved with his scene partners. That's when things come alive, and *change.* Because that's when input other than that which has come solely from his own work comes into play to help shape, not only the role of each character, but the play as a whole. Until his character is in relationship with the other characters, not even his own character is fully embodied. Till he is actually "living on stage" with his scene partners, he is but one facet of an un-realized reality—a politician with no constituency, a family man with no family; he is a character with no play. But as he interacts with and is affected by others, he becomes able to "perform" or *live* his drama on stage.

The public speaker doesn't have "rehearsal" per se, in that he doesn't rehearse with his scene partners—his audience. He spends all of his "rehearsal" or prac-tice time privately devoted to his speech, becoming more purposeful about what he means to say. Then he, too, may think he is set—until he steps up to the podium. Then things change for him as well. Before, it was all him—he was in his shower, undisturbed—singing an aria. Now he is facing a concert hall filled with raw energy in the form of other viewpoints and opinions and judgments and questions that interrupt and challenge—that affect—the speech he thought, in a vacuum, he was ready to give. This happens to the speaker, however, not in the safe space of a rehearsal, as it does with an actor, but "on the spot" during his performance.

In the case of you the speaker, then, you need to train yourself in your "rehearsal" to customize your speech to each new audience, as you find necessary, as well as to remain flexible to roll with the surprising punches. But look at the power in that!

2. The opportunity to increase your confidence.

Most of us come to the point of confidence slowly, line upon line, by just putting our attention on our work, and practicing—by rehearsing. Devoting time and attention to your work, you build your expertise as well as your sense of authority, and you eventually deem yourself worthy of success. You self-empower. This is building on a solid foundation.

Don't be afraid to self-talk, to self-encourage. Remind yourself on a regular basis that you are good—in all that that means. Tell yourself you are talented and then get out there and demonstrate that. Tell yourself that you are beautiful or handsome—or both! And then dress and carry yourself as a beautiful, handsome person. You're not a child any longer; you have to do this for yourself. And don't rely on a lover. Remember that you have a holy work to perform. No matter how big or small, _it counts_. You are increasing understanding in our world; you are decreasing fear and anxiety. Acknowledge this in your private rehearsal preparation time.

Prep + Love = Confidence

The great prize in this world is peace of mind. Your desire to do a good job and help others puts you "in service," which makes you humble, which makes you feel in synchronicity with the universe and its work for the day, _Hi-Ho!_ Which makes you feel safe and at peace.

3. The opportunity to experiment.

Allow yourself to experiment in your rehearsals. _Make_ yourself improvise. There's no technique like it to ground you in the feeling that you know your territory and will be able to handle it if you "forget your lines." Go wild! Get "off script." Come out of the box. This is what rehearsal is for, and it is the place for it, whether with others or alone—to make a fool of yourself, to go too far, to fall on your bottom. All of which you will find you can survive without dissolving into a puddle of insecurity and self-condemnation, which is the point. And you will become bolder! Which is *really* the point!

ACTING TIP:
SPEND SOME TIME WITH THE
"PICTURE OF SUCCESS."

---

4. The opportunity to develop effective body language.

Another thing you can do in rehearsal to develop and master your speech is to allow yourself to use your body language more effectively. Be *big*! And that's what it will seem like to you at first! You'll be sure that you are way over the top with your huge, exaggerated gesturing and speaking. But that's what we want! We're breaking through barriers!

Sometimes the speaker feels like he is shrink-wrapped! Like his arms are wrapped to his torso and his legs are wrapped together, with cellophane. OK, he can wiggle his fingers and toes, and nod his head, and give us a half-baked smile, but that's about it! Have you ever felt like that? Horrible, right? Well, it's horrible for the audience watching you, too! You're not doing us any favors by keeping contained and playing small—perhaps because you're afraid of being ridiculed; perhaps because you don't want to make too much of yourself.

Well, give us a break, please! *Breathe*, for heaven's sake! Stretch out! See how far this thing called your "body" can go! Try speaking with double volume. Make your gestures ridiculously large. Stomp your foot and twirl at the end of each sentence.

This is just for rehearsal, to expand your parameters, stretch your limits. You're not going to do any of this stuff in your actual performances, when you are actually addressing the board of directors, right?

Wrong! And this is the fun part. You will discover in this process of loosening up and stretching out that some of those way-too-big gestures are not really too big after all. Granted, they seem humongous to a shrink-wrapped person, especially when the spotlight (mostly of his own insecure self-attention) is on him. But *you* have freed yourself through your experimentation! *You* are free now to punctuate your speech with appropriate, definite—easy-to-read—body language. And you may dial your gestures-volume up or down, according to your own discretion. What you are heading for is the complete freedom to allow your body to gesture normally, which it does naturally when we don't interfere with it and either direct or stop it. Just be who you are. We will love you for it, because that's what we're all trying to do. And we need role models like you to help give us the courage to do it.

5. The opportunity to learn to calm and steady your voice.

Learn to calm and steady your voice. There is nothing so comforting and encouraging as a peaceful speaking voice. It dissolves panic and anxiety. It sets the tone in the room, whether it's the rehearsal room or the auditorium or theater. It's good for us all. But it's even better for you—the one who has developed enough control over her own thinking to stay cool, to keep it *real*, and not flip out and go running amok, causing chaos and nervous breakdowns wherever she goes.

The best way to achieve this calm steadiness is—as it is with so many things in life—simply, to try to. Try to make your voice smooth and even, even though it sounds shaky to you, even though you feel nervous inside. Speak right on through the shakes and try to concentrate more on what you are saying. Your voice—then your body, then your mind—will soon follow suit and settle down.

6. The opportunity to block your action.

Blocking, as an acting term, means the determining of the physical positioning and action of the actors during a performance. Blocking is the "hit your marks" portion of Spencer Tracy's famous definition of what acting requires of its practitioners, "Hit your marks and say your lines." Blocking—directing its movement—is the dance aspect of acting or speaking, just as rhythm and tonality constitute their musical aspect. The collective activity of the one collective body on stage constitutes the piece's *blocking*.

The speaker often stays fixed at the podium. But you don't have to. You, actually, have quite a bit of flexibility in your movement "on stage." And your presentation gains by your fluidity. Speakers stay at the podium, most often, because they are afraid they'll lose concentration and, therefore, control if they move around. But if what you are saying is punctuated by your appropriate expressions and gestures, your actions will help ground you in "the moment," making you even more stable and comfortable.

Experiment with your blocking. Try standing just at a podium. Then try holding a mike and walking around. Try using a prop or two to illustrate a point; perhaps including a member of your audience. Try sitting with your audience in a circle or on some other equal-playing-field level. Just be sure that whatever blocking you do is in service to the ideas in your speech, not in any way contrary to them. No unnecessary movement is of value. But neither is just standing there with your hands in your pockets like a shrink-wrapped person because you're afraid to loosen up and be fabulous!

affirmation:

I am a good, hardworker.

The Three Crucial Skills

There are three particular skills that I feel are crucial in helping a presenter feel competent and confident during his rehearsals, auditions and performances. They are:

1. The craft of cold reading.
2. The ability to memorize.
3. The ability to improvise.

Technique #13:
LEARNING THE CRAFT OF COLD READING

It is imperative for an actor to have a good, solid cold reading technique because, as a rule, he secures his acting jobs in one of two ways—through performing a monologue or by cold reading "sides"— portions of a script that he may be seeing for the first time (which is what makes his reading "cold." And most of the time it is through reading. He is given a piece of text to read, "And...action!" the director or casting director says. And if the poor actor doesn't have a good reading technique he will bob his head up and down— sea-sickeningly to those observing him—between his page and the eyes of his reading partner, with plenty of errors and little appropriate feeling along the way. Not swift. But there is a way to read that keeps the actor feeling in control and allows the director to see him interpreting the role. This way is my cold reading technique.

The same need applies to you, the speaker, especially with regards to spur-of-the-moment speeches. You may be given a page or two of text and asked, "Will you please get up and read this?" And if you don't know how to deal agilely with the material you are given to read, you may feel and come off as stiff and uncertain, unable to read it with any degree of dominion. Again, enter my cold reading technique.

First of all, always get the sides early if you can—the day before, or even a half hour before your audition or performance. (Then you won't have to read it *cold* inside.) But if you can't, or if just before show-time your employer springs it on you that, actually, you seem more suited to read something different from what you prepared, here is the technique:

MY "COLD READING" TECHNIQUE

Silently read a short sentence or a phrase that breaks naturally (at an *and*, a *but*, or a comma, for example) like it would in natural conversation then look up at your scene partner and say it. (Repeat:) Look back down at your text for the next phrase or short sentence then look up at your partner and say it.

And that's it! It's as simple as that! Simple, *but not easy.* Not until you have practiced and built the skill. But once you get it, it's great! What you are doing is capturing into your short term memory a portion of the text—colored by your snap judgment of what it means—and delivering it that way to your scene partner, or audience. You read it silently. But when you are speaking, you are speaking with your eyes off the page and on your partner. You look down, capture a short piece of it into your mind then look up and say it.

EXERCISE:

"Practicing Cold Reading." Let's practice cold reading. (First, let me lay in some text that we can use as sample text—a portion of The Grimms' Tale, *SNOW WHITE.)*

OUR SAMPLE TEXT PIECE #1: *"SNOW WHITE"*

Once in midwinter when the snowflakes were falling from the sky like feathers, a queen sat sewing at a window with an ebony frame. And as she was sewing and looking out at the snowflakes, she pricked her finger with her needle and three drops of blood fell on the snow. The red looked so beautiful on the white snow that she thought to herself: "If only I had a child as white as snow and as red as blood and as black as the wood of my window frame." A little while later she gave birth to a daughter, who was as white as snow and as red as blood, and her hair was as black as ebony. They called her Snow White.

Let's work with just that much. Begin: Read a portion of the first sentence silently to see where a good place to break is. How about: *"Once in midwinter when the snowflakes were falling from the sky like feathers,"*?

Well, it has a comma, and it breaks where we might naturally break in normal conversation, but it is way too long to remember effortlessly, which is what we are going for. (You will build your capacity slowly.)

Try again. Natural pauses happen in two shorter places:
1. *"Once"*
2. *"Once in midwinter"*

Those are your choices. I'd say your best choice is: *"Once in midwinter . . ."*

Ready? Let's try it. And remember, don't speak until you've made the capture into your short term memory and your eyes are off the page (and on your partner). Here we go:

Silently read the words, *"Once in midwinter."* Good. Now look up and say them. Good. Now look back down and silently read the words, *"when the snowflakes were falling from the sky like feathers."* Now look up and say them . . .

And there you have it! That's the idea. And if you're reading with someone else, when it's the other person's turn to read, mark your place with your finger and give the other person "eyes." Then when it's your turn to speak again, look down at that place where your finger is, capture the next short piece of it into short term memory, then look up and say it to your partner. Don't try to get your next line ahead of time, though. You want to speak your lines as an honest reaction to what your partner says to you.

I'm sure you can see that this is a great skill for a speaker to develop. You will be able to read from a piece of text— any piece of text—without looking like you are reading the whole time. And all this skill requires for you to master it is a little practice. Pretty soon you'll be able, with just a quick sweep of a glance, to pick up a few words and then deliver them with mastery. Do take the time to learn this skill well. It can be of use to you in many areas in your life. When the criminal is screeching away, you can be the one who captured the license plate number. And when the policeman asks, "Are you sure that that was the number?" you can say with assurance, "Oh, yes, officer, I'm sure!"

Technique #14:

LEARNING HOW TO MEMORIZE

Let me put your mind at rest about something right now. If you have any fear that you don't have what it takes to memorize, or you can't memorize well, or that it's just too hard to memorize, you *do*, you *can*, and it is *not*! You just need a few pointers, and it is my pleasure to give them to you. Nor—and this is big, too—do you have to perform until you are ready! So don't worry.

Ideally, the purpose of memorization is to help you capture the words of your speech into your memory so concretely that the audience will believe that you are speaking (and *meaning*) them off the top of your head for the first time. You want to have the words so solidly committed to memory that, number one, they seem impromptu, and, number two, you could truly say them a different—but equally effective—way every performance. The words are not fully memorized until then. There are no blank or weak spots. Your vision is complete. As you are saying one line the next line is already unfolding before you in your mind like a strait, unobstructed road that you are effortlessly traveling. This is the ideal. So how do we achieve it?

DON'T MEMORIZE TOO EARLY

First and foremost, avoid the temptation to memorize your lines too soon. Memorizing too soon is one of the biggest mistakes an actor or speaker can make. You do not get the cookie in acting or speaking for knowing your lines. You get the cookie for feeling the feelings. So don't commit your lines to memory until you have consciously determined *how* they should be committed. Because the part of the mind that memorizes is like a copy machine. You want to have everything in order and in proper relationship to everything else before you fix it in memory. If you copy the way you say your words *out of order*, it is only going to be harder to rearrange them later.

When you have become able to read your speech, from the page, exactly as you would like to be able to deliver it once you have memorized it, then, and only then, are you ready to commit it to memory. In other words, you should be able to read the speech over the phone to someone and the person on the other end of the line shouldn't be able to tell that you're reading it, because it is coming off your tongue so naturally. That's when you're ready to "memorize." And because you will have done your preparation work so thoroughly, a great gift will be yours in the fact that, by that time, you will already have much of it memorized. And you will be much less likely to forget your lines during your performances because you will be so certain where you are. Plus, you will be able to vamp! (Which follows below.) All of which will combine to lessen your chances of being afflicted by that blinding mental horror, *stage fright!* So how do we memorize a speech once we're ready to do so?

How to Memorize—Ten Easy Steps

Let's use the same portion of text from SNOW WHITE to work with:

Our Sample Text Piece #1: *"SNOW WHITE"*

Once in midwinter when the snowflakes were falling from the sky like feathers, a queen sat sewing at a window with an ebony frame. And as she was sewing and looking out at the snowflakes, she pricked her finger with her needle and three drops of blood fell on the snow. The red looked so beautiful on the white snow that she thought to herself: "If only I had a child as white as snow and as red as blood and as black as the wood of my window frame." A little while later she gave birth to a daughter, who was as white as snow and as red as blood, and her hair was as black as ebony. They called her Snow White.

1. Read the text aloud ten times. If you're doing this already, fine. If not, you might do so now. You want to become very familiar with the words in your mouth. Get comfortable with them. Read with a lot of awareness. As I mentioned earlier, you'll find things in reading #7 that went right by you in reading #5.

2. Look up all the words you don't know. This sounds obvious but you'd be surprised how many speakers simply speak or recite a word they've never even heard before, just to sail past it. It's laziness. How many times have you come to a word in a book and you've thought to yourself, "I should look this up in the dictionary," but didn't? I'm guilty of it, believe me. Well, when you are about to be speaking the words on stage or at the podium you cannot indulge yourself in such carelessness. (What if someone in your audience asks you for a definition?!) We're depending on you to tell us the truth.

3. Have a meaning for everything you say. Knowing what every word that you utter *means*, is crucial to your having a meaning for everything that you say. And in order to speak with the deep passion that is the only thing that makes speaking truly worth the effort, you need to really mean it. (Which you can't do unless you thoroughly know what you mean.)

4. Know your main points (super-objective). This is the guiding light, the light on the miner's hat, that keeps you on track. It is the answer to the question, "What am I trying to say, here?" It reminds you where you are in your speech at any given moment.

5. Paraphrase. Become so familiar with the material that you can put the whole speech in your own (or *other*) words. Try this: Read a line of text, aloud, then say it in a different way—using different words—while maintaining the same core meaning. This gives you a sense of mastery over that material—and enables you to improvise, if necessary.

FOR EXAMPLE:

Paraphrase: *"A little while later she gave birth to a daughter, who was as white as snow and as red as blood, and her hair was as black as ebony."* You might say, *"Not long thereafter, she had a daughter who looked just as she had envisioned her."*

6. Read it as if it were memorized. Again, Become so comfortable and facile with the material and how you want to deliver it that you can read it exactly the way you would deliver it if you had it perfectly memorized. Now you are ready to memorize!
7. Memorize word clusters first. Instead of starting at the beginning with word one: "Once in midwinter…" go through the piece in search of "word clusters" and get them memorized, so they won't hang you up when you come to them later.

FOR EXAMPLE:

"snowflakes were falling from the sky like feathers," "three drops of blood fell on the snow," and *"as white as snow and as red as blood and as black as the wood of my window frame."*

8. Memorize completely. Now go back to the beginning and start with word one. Don't worry—it's going to fall right into place now. Take your time. Enjoy it!
9. Reinforce joints and weak spots. ou've got it just about memorized now, right? You recite it again, and you've almost got it—there are just a few places where you get tripped up, or you falter. This is normal

but it needs special attention. Instead of going back to the beginning and starting over each time, spend some concentrated time in the rough areas.

FOR EXAMPLE:

Let's say you make it the first few lines, past the point where you say, *" . . . and three drops of blood fell on the snow."* Good. But you falter with the next line: *"The red looked so beautiful on the white snow . . ."* You might instruct yourself to see that the drops of blood that fell on the snow were a *beautiful red*, which may cue you that *"The red looked so beautiful . . ."* And off you go. Experiment; find little tricks and reminders that work for you.

10. Speed recite. Good! Now you've really got it down, right? Not quite, not until you can speed recite it. Sit in a still spot, focus your eyes on some still object (a vase, a tree) and quietly, but aloud, recite your piece as fast as you can. When you can recite it pretty darned fast with no mistakes, you've got it memorized. Hooray!

A Note

A note here, though. Your memorization of a piece is only temporary. Unless you recite it regularly (daily, for most of us), you will begin to forget your piece.

Stay Open

I have found that this method of memorization works well for most of my acting students and my speech clients, and I hope it will help you. But, as in everything I and your other teachers and coaches recommend, it all comes down to what works most effectively for you. Try this method, but do stay open to others' tips and guidelines as well.

EXERCISE:

"Practicing Memorization." Use the above steps as a guide for effective and tension-free memorization.

affirmation:

I have a great memory.

Don't Hurry It—Don't Worry It

An important key to successful memorization is, *don't hurry!* Do not try to "get the dang thing memorized as soon as possible!" Take your time with it.Take it from being a chore to being a delight by playing with it. Memorization can really be quite fun. Give yourself plenty of time and memorize just a bit at a time. The fun comes in the mastery of it, and mastery comes with time and attention to detail. Start to get the music of it going in your recitation—the rhythm, the pacing, the dynamics of it. Piece it together like a puzzle. Keep the process tension-free.

Most of the time, I find that the horror of memorization stems from some nightmare juvenile experience when the child stood up to recite and he wasn't prepared. He wasn't ready, and some thoughtless teacher may even have rubbed his nose in it. So, naturally, his experience was a miserable one. But there is an easy two-part fix to that problem: spend more time preparing, and don't get up to perform until you are ready to. That's it! So no problem. Update the ol' mental files: "I do *not* hate memorizing. I am *not* afraid that I can't do it. I *can* do it. Bring it on!"

Technique #15:
LEARNING HOW TO IMPROVISE

There are so many different ways to improvise. By definition, in fact, an infinite number of ways. Some of them we've already discussed. Some others might include: Deliver your speech one time as if you were a ten year old child. Then, perhaps, once as if you were the most impatient woman in the world! Try performing different actions while delivering your speech, such as washing the dishes, or eating grapes, or ironing a shirt. This can be so much fun! Try whatever

117

occurs to you (as long as it's legal and nobody gets hurt!) You might just land on some idea or method that helps you to deliver your speech exactly the way you would like to. Speaking very loudly, speaking in another accent, speaking as if everything you are saying is a lie, or speaking very softly as if you are on a bus talking to the person next to you and want to keep your conversation private.

The main point of improvising is to loosen you up, break you apart and get you "out of the box," out of the "right way" of doing something—into *your* way of doing it. As Andre Gide said, you've got to let go of the shore for a long while if you expect to discover new land. Upon which you may then reassemble your presentation more in the way that you want it to be.

So how does the speaker improvise? You improvise by saying "yes" in your prep to the different modes and means of delivery of your speech—especially the unlikely ones— that occur to you. To what end? To help you find the most effective way to deliver your speech, and to increase your confidence that you can't be thrown (very far!) by anything, including forgetting your lines.

As a reward for your courage and willingness, here is a "super tool" that will help you any time you do think you have lost your place during your presentation. It is called "vamping," or "vamping in place."

Technique #16:

VAMPING IN PLACE

"Vamping" is a dance term. It means "dancing in place." The dancer stays in the same place for a minute, going from one foot to the other, until she moves forward again. It's like "dog-paddling" or treading water in a pool. It keeps you moving, keeps you afloat, but it doesn't move you forward. It does, however, keep you from coming to a stop, which is its purpose. "Vamping," the great savior of the terrified "line-forgetter!" Well, be terrified no longer!

As I'm sure you know, there is nothing scarier on stage or at the podium than that moment when, although you did your prep, you suddenly forget your lines. Faces turn red, eyes pop widely, hearts race (or stop!) saliva does something unseemly, and one cannot swallow. These things ought not to be! Can't anybody do something?! Yes! Yes! We hear you and we're trying to get through, here! We have the solution for you! We have the technique that we call "vamping!"

IN ESSENCE, THE TECHNIQUE IS THIS:

MY "VAMPING IN PLACE" TECHNIQUE

As soon as you realize that you are in trouble—that you've lost your place or forgotten your line—improvise by talking a little bit more about what you've just said.

That's it! O.K., let's try it, so you'll know what I mean. Let's use another portion of text from *SNOW WHITE*:

OUR SAMPLE TEXT PIECE #2: *"SNOW WHITE"*

Meanwhile, the poor child was all alone in the great forest. She was so afraid that she looked at all the leaves on the trees and didn't know what to do. She began to run, she ran over sharp stones and through brambles, and the wild beasts passed by without harming her. She ran as long as her legs would carry her and then, just before nightfall, she saw a little house and went in to rest.

OK, that's your text. And you are rolling along and you say, *"She began to run, she ran over sharp stones and through brambles, and the wild beasts passed by without harming her,"* and this is where you forget your lines. So you vamp. You stay right where you are, right where you've forgotten, and just "talk a little bit more about what you've just said."

Something like:

"All kinds of beasts, some she'd never seen before. They were running too, running past her, faster than she could run . . ."

119

Do you notice what is happening? Your vamping is leading you right back on track.

"But she didn't stop; she didn't give up," you continue. And this cues you! Magically, you remember, and say, back on script, *"She ran as long as her legs would carry her..."*

Only, it isn't magic. It's fabulous, but it isn't magic. By continuing to talk about what you've just said, that part of the mind that is secure and always knows what is happening will not only lead you to a word or phrase that will trigger your memory and lead you back on cue, but your landing will be charged with an extra-emotional kick that punches up the excitement in the scene (after all, for a second you were hanging by a thread!), which you will have earned by having thoroughly done your armchair/preparation work.

Once you master this technique of vamping, you will never again fear that you will forget your lines. At least, not nearly so intensely. Because you will know that, if you do, you have sure salvation. Henceforth, you will always feel safe on stage. The technique will also help you eliminate your resistance to memorizing—if there be any—because there won't be as much at stake if you forget your lines; you will be able to vamp!

THE IMPORTANCE OF THOROUGH REHEARSAL

Alfred Hitchcock said he made his films before he ever shot the first frame. He imagined, and story-boarded, and edited them, all in his head, before he actually did so on film. Hitchcock did his preparation work. Certainly there were changes and differences between prep and production, but he was prepared to accommodate them. Did that preparation diminish his creativity, do you think? I don't think so. And Hitchcock didn't think so. On the contrary, he felt being so prepared was what freed him to be more creative on the set during production than he would have been if he hadn't relieved himself of the many details that he'd taken care of in prep: lengths of shots, lenses, angles, and so on. He could focus on performances, and be free and ready to take advantage of the "happy accidents" that occur during shooting.

Technique #17:
PRACTICE! PRACTICE! PRACTICE!

Like the film director and the actor, the public speaker has a big job to do. And big jobs take lots of work. Hard work, smart work—and practice.

Practice rehearsing your speech as much as your schedule will allow. Don't worry that you might over-practice. That's like beginning musicians who are afraid they will erode their creativity if they learn to read music. They won't. And you won't spend all of your creative thunder by practice. Besides, every time you step up to the podium before a new audience, it is a new ball game. So practice as much as you can and feel good about it.

Schedule Your Practice Sessions As Definitely As Your Performances

I enjoy writing songs and performing them, and when I have a performance coming up, I schedule my rehearsals very strictly. I start three weeks out. Every day during the three weeks leading up to show time, I vocalize and play (guitar) and run my set of songs, twice. If I have other musicians joining me, I bring them on board for two or three rehearsals the last week. So, to me, my show isn't forty-five minutes long; my show is three weeks long! And, although my listeners wouldn't, I enjoy every minute of it because I have learned to love the prep—as shaky as things may seem at the start. And by the time it is show time, it's an easy day for me—I only have to do the show once! And I'm very comfortable with the material by then. That day, I just run my set one time—on stage as the performance.

Thank You, Bert

I had occasion to spend some time with Bert Jansch and some other wonderful musicians over the summer in England some years ago. Bert taught me a beautiful lesson. We were all staying on a large estate together. My bedroom was on the same floor as Bert's. When I was walking by his room one morning, I saw him sitting on his bed with his guitar. This was not unusual. He invited me in. In the course of our visit I asked him if he ever got tired of practicing. He laughed and said, "I don't practice very often." I said, "But it seems like you're always practicing. Like now. You've always got your guitar with you." He said, "When I'm alone and it seems to you that I'm practicing, that's when I'm really playing. When I'm up on stage or in the studio playing with others, I approach it as if I'm only practicing."

Perform, play, practice! Spend time and get good at your work. Do it for *you*—*and* for others. Get to the point where, when somebody says you are a really great speaker, you nod inside as you say, "Thank you." It's just a fact, after all. You are a really great speaker. And you have the calluses on your soul to prove it.

> ## ACTING TIP:
> KNOW THAT YOU ARE THOROUGHLY
> PREPARED AND REHEARSED.

Technique #18:
  NEVER WING IT! (*UNLESS YOU HAVE TO!*)

No matter how much you prepare and rehearse, you can never anticipate all the surprises that can pop up during a live performance. Here's a secret: don't fight it. There's nothing more fun for a performer than having to "wing it" when you are well-rehearsed and prepared to do so! It's wonderfully exciting when something "goes wrong," *if* you are prepared— if you know where you are in the piece, where it went wrong, and how to get back on track! If, however, you aren't prepared when things go kerflooey, there's nothing scarier.

Never "wing it" on purpose, however. In other words, never get up on stage unprepared. Beforehand, while the pressure is off, you may think you'll be able to wing it, no problem. But when you get on stage you'll feel more nervous and less in control. If it's a spur of the moment thing, a task or an opportunity offered to you to speak off the cuff, and you feel equal to it, fine. But don't be cavalier. Don't take off in an airplane until you know how to fly it, because you will crash. But once you do know how to fly it, trust yourself and your skills that you will be able to handle the challenges to its safe flight and landing.

SUMMARY OF MAIN POINTS

1. Good rehearsals provide great opportunities for the speaker:
   a. To learn to roll with the punches
   b. To increase his confidence
   c. To experiment
   d. To develop effective body language
   e. To calm and steady his voice
   f. To block his action
2. Prep + Love = Confidence
3. Every speaker should develop the three crucial skills:
   a. The craft of cold reading
   b. The ability to memorize
   c. The ability to improvise
4. Learn to "vamp in place."
5. Practice! Practice! Practice!
6. Never wing it! (Unless you have to!)

CHAPTER EIGHT

Techniques for Relaxing and Warming Up

> "The true orator speaks with his entire personality, with all
> the powers of his being, and for that reason, at the moment
> just preceding his address, he should summon, and marshal,
> and concentrate all his instruments."
>
> —*The Art of Extempore Speaking* by M. Bautai

Why is it that some of the most important things in life
are the very things that we think we don't have time for? We
don't have enough time for our kids, for our spouses, for our
parents. We haven't time to watch the sunset today, or to take
a look at the full moon tonight—never mind that it will be
raining for the next five days and that the moon won't be full
again for a month. Or to make a smoothie instead of grabbing
a candy bar. Or to meditate, or pray. We know we should but
we don't. We're busy. We're working on it, though, right?

Yes, we are. And we need to keep working on it because
relaxing and warming up your body and preparing yourself
mentally before you step onto the platform to perform is one of
those important composite activities that you, the speaker, must
continue to work *not* to forego. No matter how busy you are
or how unnecessary, or *luxurious*, it seems to you, you cannot
afford to forego it—if you want to have the optimum speaking
experience. Oh, sure, you can squeak by without it. But you
won't feel centered and ready, and as worthy of a fabulous,
successful experience as you would if you'd warmed up. Because, just as your armchair prep work is crucial to reaching
the depth of your performance content, relaxation and warming
up are crucial to your smooth delivery of it. It gets the jitters
out (at least under control), focuses the mind, and centers you
in your soul-purpose for the performance. When you decide,

deliberately, to relax and warm up, you leave your past outside and enter your new present, as if you are passing through a mental vestibule of preparation.

Technique #19:
   ENTERING THE VESTIBULE OF PREPARATION

Often, in colder climates, houses and commercial buildings have small entry rooms or vestibules that people enter first before then proceeding into the main house or building. The vestibule is a passage area, a protective preparatory way to keep the cold out of the main buildings.

I think of the relaxation and other exercises that an actor or speaker does before performing as a sort of vestibule through which he or she passes from his daily life into the world of his performance. This vestibule includes physical relaxation and warm-up, breathing exercises, a vocal warm-up, and—most important—a mental warm-up, by which the performer recognizes and honors the task he or she is about to undertake. The vestibule is the place where you brush off the dust of your daily life before you step into your art. You are embarking on an important work when you speak—the merchandise you are dealing with is truth and, naturally, you will want to prepare for that work as seriously and reverently as possible. But the main purpose of going into the vestibule is to prepare yourself so that you, the speaker, will enjoy your experience to the fullest. Only then will you best benefit your listeners.

> **ACTING TIP:**
> BE PREPARED. REMAIN IN CONTROL
> BUT BE READY TO IMPROVISE.

Technique #20:
   ALWAYS TAKE THE TIME

I don't believe in spending a lot of time in the vestibule—just enough to warm you up, not wear you out or put you to sleep! But to become calm and focused, you do have to take a moment or two to step into your speaking work.

But what if you're really in a hurry? You have five minutes to get home from work, take a shower, get dressed, and drive thirty minutes to the venue. How are you going to find the time to warm up? You simply don't have it, right?

No, that is not right. We *do* have time, despite appearances. If we make the effort to prepare ourselves—if for only two minutes—we will find that we will have gained at lease the two minutes back because we will now be working more efficiently.

Technique #21:
RELAXATION, BREATHING
AND VOCAL EXERCISES*

Below are a few examples of physical relaxation, breathing, and vocal warm-up exercises. You'll find that I have mixed the categories together so that the work doesn't become academic or laborious. Try a few. Mix and match as you like.

1. Ten Breath/Hear Release. Take in a nice deep breath. Hold it for a count of ten. Release it all at once with a good, strong, indulgent sound of relief. Do ten .
2. Universal Hug. Imagine you are standing outside. Reach your arms up to the sky for a huge helping of symbols that, to you, represent happiness and abundance: *dollar signs, hearts, flowers, candy canes, awards, music symbols*—whatever works for you; hug a big portion of them to your chest, and smile with gratitude.
3. *Some of these exercises were first offered in my book, Acting From a Spiritual Perspective.*
4. The Five-Minute Five-Step Prep.
    a. Baby cries. Take a deep breath and then, from deep down, cry out "waah!" as if you are a hungry little baby unself-consciously wailing for his nourishment. Do it three times. On the third become impatient, angry even, and pulse out the wail: "Waa-ah-ah!"

b. Find the center. Find the soft, sweet place of privacy in your consciousness and mentally place it somewhere in your body—your chest, your solar plexus, the back of your head. Breathe deeply into that place, holding your breath and attention there for a count of ten, calming and centering yourself a little more with each full breath. Do it five times.

c. Relax and go limp. Keeping your breathing slow and constant, do a slow neck roll, first to the left, then to the right. Then, in the following order, tighten and release—one at a time—your face, shoulders, arms, hands, back, and legs: Tighten the muscles and hold them taut for ten seconds, then drop, shake, and relax them. Be thorough.

d. Five consonants. This is a vocal warm-up. Choose five consonants. For example: K, L, B, D, R. Place a wine cork between your teeth and then, as clearly as possible, speak loudly the five vowels, each preceded by each of the consonants: kay, kee, ki, ko, ku; lay, lee, lie, lo, lu; and so on. This effectively opens the back of the throat.

e. Find the center again. Repeat step "b" above. Find your center again and focus your breath and attention there for a count of ten, calming yourself more deeply with each full breath. Do it five times, then end the exercise with a short silent affirmation that acknowledges the importance of, and your ability to do, the work you are about to undertake.

5. The Chair Caveman-Emote Relaxation. Sit in an armless straight-back chair. Starting with the head, tighten, hold, shake, and then relax all the major muscle groups (head and neck, shoulders, arms and hands, back and abdominals, buttocks, and legs and feet). At the same time, pretend that you are a caveman—or woman—and, using deep breaths and loud wordless vocal sounds, express at least five major emotions, such as fear, anger, joy, love, and envy as you release. Translated into sounds as you relax each group, the breath may sound

like "aah!" (fear), "ehh-yehh-yehh!" (anger), "ooh!" (joy), "mmmm," (love), and "puh-huh!" (envy) as you let the breath go.

6.   The Public Chair Grounding. This is a short, almost silent warm-up that you can do while you are sitting backstage before your presentation.

Breathing deeply, slowly use your fingertips to massage the muscles of your face (jaws, temples, forehead), the back of your neck, and your shoulders. Then extend your arms out sideways, shoulder height, leave them there until they burn, then cross them across your chest until you are hugging your opposite shoulders. Open them up and cross them the other way, hugging the opposite shoulders.

Next, extend and tighten the muscles in your legs. Release. Flex your feet. Release. Rotate your ankles. Then fold your torso down until it is lying over your thighs, your hands on the ground, your head hanging limp between your knees. Breathe deeply. Slowly roll up.

7.   Additional Warm-Up Suggestions:

   a.   The Yeah-Yeah Breath. Take a deep breath and pulse it out in short bursts by repeating the word *yeah* until the breath is completely used up. This is an affirmation as well as a breathing exercise. Yeah! Do three of them.

   b.   Fake Laughter. Start out faking it until you begin to buy it! Feed it until it begins to feel natural and you are laughing your fool head off! It feels wonderful to the body and the mind (and is terrific proof that you are always in control of your emotions.)

   c.   The Varying Ten-Breath Chant. Take in a breath, then release it using a particular sound pattern until the breath is used up. Do this ten times, but each time use a different sound pattern on the exhale. If you are doing the chant with others, you might use the same pattern all ten times, as they might consistently use theirs. The important thing is to listen and relate to one another while, at the same time, maintaining your individuality.

Technique #22:

MORE VOCAL TECHNIQUES

1. Speak *up!* The importance of effective projection. The most important goal of all vocal technique is to make sure that the speaker is heard! This seems obvious, but you'd be surprised how often a speaker, an actor—anyone on stage—must be coached during rehearsals or practice sessions, or sound check sessions, to *"Please speak up! We can't hear you!"* The main reason for this is that the speaker thinks he is talking plenty loud enough as it is. This is because when you, the speaker, are on the hot seat, you are, quite naturally, more self-conscious. You're more aware of yourself, more tuned in to yourself, so you're hearing yourself more acutely; you are *standing out in the mix*, so to speak, to yourself. Therefore, you think you are talking louder than you are, so you lower your vocal volume.

But we don't hear you that way. On the contrary, we need you to speak up so that we can more easily pick you out from the rest of the sounds in the mix. This helps us concentrate on what you have to say. So do us a favor—a service, really. Get over being self-conscious. Meet *our* needs, and *speak up*! Because if we can't hear you, your efforts—and value to us—are zilch!

2. Speak in your right vocal register. Here's a good rule of thumb for you: try to speak a little lower in your vocal register than you think is most natural to you. This is to compensate for nerves, which usually makes you raise your register a bit. Sometimes more than a bit.

In a nutshell, you can speak from your throat, from your chest, or from your upper belly. The majority of people speak from their upper chest, with some throat thrown in. The mobster molls—Judy Holiday in _Born Yesterday_, for instance—speak from their throats. The trained speaker, the orator, speaks from his upper belly (diaphragm) and lower chest.

When an actor is playing a character, he or she selects a vocal register he thinks is appropriate to the character, which will help define the character's place of origin, social status, and educational background. A _speaker_ defines himself or herself—he is his own character. He is free to adopt whatever register he chooses. To my ear, and I think to most peoples', the voice sounds more cultured, as well as more grounded, when it has a bit of bass (diaphragm or lower chest) in it. And, again, it will always rise somewhat when the speaker is feeling nervous. So slow down when performing, speak a little more deeply than usual, and you'll be good to go.

> 3. Dynamics and variety. A friend of mine who plays guitar for me sometimes is always reminding me to be mindful of the dynamics in my vocals. He's talking about the highs and the lows, the soft and the loud, even the white spaces of silence at times, as well as the hurry-up speed sometimes necessary to catch up and compensate for the rests. He's talking about a little variety—please, God—could it not be _boring_?!

A speaker, so he doesn't put his audience to sleep—so he actually communicates something to them, let alone _moves_ them to action—has to be particularly aware of and orchestrate his vocal dynamics. The speaker deals with this the way a choreographer designs a dance. Maybe you start out with a bang, an attention-getter. Then maybe you speak as softly as you can _while still being heard,_ and then raise your voice to a more normal volume. Experiment with this. Try a few different combinations of dynamics to see which ones most effectively help you achieve your speaking objectives.

> 4. Diction: pronunciation and enunciation. Those of us who have studied Lee Strasberg's method of acting training know that there is nothing in his

teachings that advocates endeavoring to be verbally unintelligible. That cliché notion of Marlon Brando as the typical "method" actor who is little more than an intentional word-slurring blubber-puss is highly exaggerated. His words, as we have record of them, were not, in fact, unintelligible, even while he was endeavoring to be as emotionally authentic as possible in his performances.

The point is valid, however, that no matter how emotionally involved the speaker is, the audience must be able to understand the words that he or she is saying. You must be heard! You must speak loudly enough, you must speak in an effective register, you must vary your dynamics in order to keep your audience's interest, and you must properly pronounce and enunciate your words. To "pronounce" them is to render them in alignment with current common usage. To "enunciate" them is to pronounce them clearly, with no vowel, nor consonant— no syllable—eluding its proper emphasis.

5. Last, but not least, eliminate all "fillers." These are the "uh's", the "um's", the "you know's," and so on. The infesting weirdness that constitutes the idiomatic neuroses of all speakers until they clean house. They've got to go! Their presence is the most obvious sign that the speaker is an amateur. How do you get rid of them? As with breaking any bad habit, you become aware that it exists, that you're doing it; you decide to eliminate it; and then you work at it. Simple, right? Yes. Easy? No so much. But if you mean it, and stick with it, you'll win.

One reason people say, "Um," between points is that they are afraid that if they are silent for a moment somebody else will grab the floor. And they're right! So they hang on the line. But you don't need to hang on the line. Say your piece then yield the floor. Your turn will come around again, when you have something else to say. Besides, you appear smarter when you don't talk too much. What is that quip? "Keep quiet and let them think you might be stupid, rather than open your mouth and remove all doubt."

---

affirmation:

I know who I am,
what my purpose is,
and that Life is seeing
to it that I succeed.

Technique #23:

THE MENTAL WARM-UP

1. Prayer. When I was writing my book, *The Actor's Quotation Book*, James Lipton invited me to attend the taping of his show, *"Inside the Actor's Studio,"* the night he interviewed Jeff Bridges. I went. Several things struck me. Bridges happens to be one of my particular heart-throbs, so *he* did. But apart from that, two other things stuck out as fascinating. One was that Bridges creates a beautiful coffee-table memorabilia book of the films he plays a major role in and gives copies of it to the cast and crew members at the end of the show. I thought that was very cool. The other was that, when Lipton asked him how he passes the hours of wait-time on a movie set (when he's not taking photos for his books), he said, "I pray a lot." He didn't define what he meant by "pray," but he'd said it with neither shyness nor any embarrassment, and I found that very fascinating.

Prayer can be a big fancy thing with all the trappings of a church, or it can be a simple request, "Please help me to do a good job." It can be a statement of trust: "I know goodness is operating." Or an expression of gratitude to "the powers that be." It can also be a trusting relinquishment of responsibility and worry along the lines of Anthony Hopkins' admitted favorite of all prayers: "F... it." However one prays, the mental act of prayer is an acknowledgment by the petitioner that he believes there exists an address-ee—powerful at least to the degree required by his petition—who he hopes is inclined to help him. He may feel he doesn't even have to ask—which is how the birds get along, I assume.

2. Meditation. You may define them differently but I see prayer as thinking good thoughts, addressing them to your sense of deity, and keeping a channel open for a response; while meditation is detaching from your thoughts, letting them go the moment you spot them in your mind. You breathe, you let go. Of what? Of reaction to the thoughts, of participating in the "drama" of life. "I hate Bob!" Let it go. Om, shanti, om. "I'm a terrible actor and I'm getting fat!" Whatever. Not my thought. Om.

Prayer and meditation both have their place and utility in helping to steady and focus the mind of the speaker before *showtime*—exactly to the degree that they do! And, to the degree *that they do*, you might use them.

ACTING TIP:
CONTROL YOUR ATTITUDE.

3. Music. Finding the right music to help you relax, or to put you in the mood of your character of "Fabulous Speaker, Speaking"—is largely a question of trial and error. The wrong music can make you feel agitated. But the right music can be very helpful.

Music is best used to *underscore* the feelings you have chosen to feel. And you do choose them, consciously or not.

We all choose the majority of our feelings all day long, more so than we realize. In our work on stage or at the podium, music should be "applied" with workman-like mindfulness. Which is to say, if you choose to feel happy, accentuate this with happy music. If you just want to relax and get peaceful before your performance, try Brahms, or Eastern Indian music. If you wish to whip yourself up into a fury, Beethoven is your man. Or Metallica.

> 4. Mantras and Affirmations. Simply, a *mantra* is a short spiritual, or positive, statement that you repeat to yourself over and over, silently or aloud, during a sitting of, say, between ten and thirty minutes, to calm and steady your thinking. Sometimes the statement is given to one by one's spiritual teacher; sometimes the person makes it up himself. Sometimes it's in the person's native language; sometimes it's in Latin or Sanskrit. A couple of examples might be: "Life is eternally perfect." "In mind, Ram (God); in the hand, work." "Beholding the Self, by the Self, one is satisfied in the Self."

Affirmations are true, positive statements one makes to oneself. "I am good." "I am talented and entitled." "I am safe and sound and protected." All of which is true spiritually, and which we are endeavoring to demonstrate more fully in our daily lives.

EXERCISE:

"Relax and Warm Up." Try the above relaxation and physical, vocal, and mental warm-up exercises and techniques to determine which ones work best for you, and then assemble a set of these as a routine for your personal use for a period of a couple of months. Then try another combination.

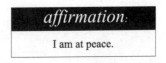

affirmation:

I am at peace.

135

SUMMARY OF MAIN POINTS

1. The vestibule of preparation is the mental place where you "take off your boots" before you embark upon your work. It includes the speaker's physical, vocal and mental warm-ups.
2. Warming-up is neither a luxury nor too time consuming. Since it prepares the speaker to work more effectively and efficiently, the speaker actually gains time by warming up. Always take the time to warm up.
3. See chapter contents for relaxation, breathing, vocal and mental exercises and Techniques.

CHAPTER NINE

In The Wings, Nearly Ready!

"Right motives give pinions to thought, and strength and freedom to speech and action."

— *Science and Health with Key to the Scriptures* by
Mary Baker Eddy

GET SET . . . !

You've found your place, done your research, created your speech or presentation, learned and practiced it, and you are warmed up and raring to go! But wait! Before you go out there, let's make sure that a few more things are in place in the way of preparation, plus get a sense of what it looks like—from the angle of the successful completion of your speech—when you are doing it right!

> **ACTING TIP:**
> ALLOW YOUR CHARACTER TO ADDRESS
> EVERY OTHER CHARACTER WITH AS MUCH
> RESPECT AS CIRCUMSTANCES WILL PERMIT.

Technique #24:
KNOWING ALL THE CHARACTERS BEFORE YOU EVER STEP ONTO THE STAGE

In the world of acting, each actor in a play or film knows every character in the play. His *character* doesn't necessarily know all the other characters, but the actor playing that character does. He's read and studied the play. He knows what his and the other characters' emotional journeys are going to be throughout the performance, he knows the actions they are going to take that will drive the play to its resolution, and he knows how the play will end. (See Technique #11: *Knowing How The Play Is Meant To End* in Chapter Six.) He knows who he is dealing with and what to expect from them. He knows all the characters before he ever steps onto the stage.

To the degree that he can implement it, this is a very useful idea for the speaker. Granted, not as many variables are *in*variable for the speaker as for the actor. The speaker knows what his character—*he*—is going to say he controls that, but he doesn't know how his scene partners—his audiences—are going to respond. Their response is not scripted and guaranteed, as it would be in a play. Nor is the outcome of the speaker's performance definite; the speaker isn't pre-provided with the security that a play's surety gives an actor. But still, there is much he can do to assure a desired outcome. To an impressive degree he, too, can know the characters in his world before he ever steps onto his stage.

Who are the characters in your, the speaker's, world? And why is it important that you *pre*-know them? Primarily, they are the ones who have sanctioned, and/or to whom you will address, your speech. To know who they are, why they asked you to speak, what they hope to get out of your presentation, and what they hope to do with it, enables you to predict what you can reasonably expect from them in the way of reaction. It's the closest you can get to the guaranteed actions and outcome an actor enjoys. But it's still not guaranteed. Anticipate, too, in fact, what you might encounter from them in the way of resistance. The point is, to the degree that you can, find out who you are dealing with so you can deal with them as cooperatively as possible to bring your speech to a successful conclusion. How do you find all this out? It can all be done with a little time and research. Interview some of them; "Google" them; find your way. One thing I can tell you for sure. Unless you do know who your listeners are and how you expect "the play" to end, it might just end a lot sooner than you thought it would! And why operate in the dark when with just a small effort you can flick on the light?

> *affirmation:*
>
> My intelligence and creative
> ability are as great
> as those of anyone who
> has ever lived.

Technique #25:

LOVE TO PERFORM!

It's a natural impulse to want to perform. It's healthy. It's a demand of the child on his parent, the student on her teacher. "Watch me! Look at me! Acknowledge that I am good, that I am fulfilling my potential, that I am pleasing you!" It starts very young. "Momma, watch me!" we call out from the diving board, the bicycle, the basketball court. "Look at me, Daddy!" we cry from the Little League diamond, the dance recital floor, the stage. And the good parent comes back immediately with acknowledgment, affirmation and encouragement—"Yes, darling, I see you and you are good! Keep going!"

If you received that kind of good, positive encouragement for your very early performances then you know how helpful it was to you in developing your courage to perform, as well as your love of performing. And I'm happy for you. But if you didn't, or didn't much, don't feel too badly or waste any more time feeling sorry for yourself about it. Most of us didn't get the fully-devoted pedigree parenting we would have liked, and our parents didn't either. They gave us some of it, they kept body and soul together, and they loved us. But you are not really at a disadvantage if you didn't have the devoted stage-father of a Mozart, because most of us didn't. The good news is, *Life* is our parent, and it is still parenting us. Life itself is still encouraging us, still watching us, cheering us onward in our endeavors. And we are still the active kids we've always been, craving to fulfill our potential.

Love to perform! Love the opportunities to be splendid! To be magnificent! To be Life's self-expression in your own

139

unique, mind-blowing way! Your love will empower and strengthen you. Enjoy expressing that power. And we will see you and tell you that you are good and cheer you on because we will recognize that goodness; we aspire to it ourselves! Credit Life for your success and then bloom! Ka*bloom*!

BUT WHAT IF YOU DON'T LOVE TO PERFORM?
(I'M JUST SAYING.)

In the hard light of speaking in public, though, how do we love to perform if we're pretty darn sure that we don't?! At least, not yet. We may *want* to love it. We may know that we've got it in us to be good speakers. That it's our destiny, even. But right now, not really so much. At all.

Like you, I recognize that as fear, fear that you don't have what it takes to meet the challenges imposed on the public speaker. Which, let's admit it, are quite demanding. As your coach, I can tell you, however—happily and confidently—that you do! You have all that it takes. Everyone does. You just need to claim that and *exercise* it. You need to *practice* that which you *choose to do*.

Technique #26:
KNOWING THAT YOU HAVE WHAT IT TAKES

YOU HAVE WHAT IT TAKES BECAUSE:

1. You have confidence! Confidence is the speaker's most important asset—real confidence, not bravado. Where does it come from? It comes from being prepared, plus passion. Remember my formula in Chapter Seven? *Preparation + love = confidence.*

2. You have humility. Humility is a light. It turns on the truth. More accurately, it turns us on to the truth. It makes the ego shut up so it can hear something besides its own propaganda. The actor who loses his humility,

his purpose on stage, loses his way in the scene. He forgets the super-objective of the scene and of the play as a whole and crashes to the level of just saying the words. He feels cut off, and he is. He wanted to stand out. And now he does, like a sore thumb.

The speaker is in even greater danger than the actor is when he fails to be humble. He's already all by himself at the podium. If he forgets that he is doing a service job and, instead, starts showing off, he'll have lost the spirit of his speech and his message will be lost to us. But you don't do that. You are humble.

3. You have passion. Being humble, however, doesn't mean that you talk so quietly that people have to yell, "We can't hear you!" and you're boring. On the contrary, you are passionate about the ideas you embrace and expound, and love. Even when you are engaged as a gun-for-hire to speak about topics that you are not personally all that passionate about, you are as passionate—as loving—as you can be. And when you can't in good conscience speak positively about a topic, or a product, you have the courage to decline the offer to speak about it at all.

4. You exercise clarity. At all times during your performance, you know the super-objective of your speech. That super-objective is the soul of your speech. It is the answer to the question that no audience member should ever have to ask: *"What in the heck is he talking about?!"* You have it together, so no one ever has to.

5. You are able to focus and concentrate. Focus: to restrict awareness to a specific set of things or ideas, dismissing all others. Concentration: to keep your awareness only there. The more specific you are about what you feel and think (not *You don't like her*

141

for some reason; but *You despise her because she ran over your parakeet!*), the more believable as a real person you are to the audience. You do this well.

6. You are observant and a good listener. Have you ever been to a theatrical performance, a play, perhaps, during which a small accident with some prop occurs and the actors "do not observe it"? For example, a woman enters the room and sets her purse on the sofa beside her. It's meant to stay there till the scene is over but this time, mid-scene, the purse falls to the floor. Everybody, on and off stage—including the actress whose purse it is—sees this happen. *The big silent gasp!* But the actress does nothing about it! The theatre is squirming with anticipation; people are thinking, "Pick it up!" But the poor actress is stuck on the way it was meant to be, ignoring what it has become. And this ruins the play—for everyone. A more experienced actor would have embraced the living aspect of that moment and turned the "happy accident" to her advantage. She might have said, "Perfect! This is exactly how my day has been going—one crash after another!" and then picked up her purse and gone on from there, to everyone's satisfaction.

That's what *you* do in your speech-making. You are aware of what's going on around you; you welcome the unexpected and you respond to it appropriately.

7. You have rhythm. I spoke about the musicality of your words in Chapter Six. You listened! You give your talks "a good beat!" It's very satisfying to us, your audience, and it helps us to learn and remember the truth in your work.

8. You remain playful and Imaginative. Which is to say, you don't take yourself or your work too seriously. You remain infused with some of the spirit

we had as kids when we "made stuff." Whether we made mud pies or little plays or we built forts, we did it *for fun*. Our needs were met by our parents or other adults, so we worked—not for a living—but for the fun of working. We still need to work that way, to at least some degree; *you do so*!

9. You stay in control. You are charged, dynamic, and determined. And more—your speech is under your relaxed and comfortable control. You claim that and you live it. Because you realize that when you speak the scepter is in your hands; the forces of the positive support you.

10. You exercise discipline. We want to work. We want to create. That's the good news. The impetus to work is strong! The also good, but not as warm and fuzzy, news is that that takes discipline! And while we're all for it right now as we consider all these ideas about good, effective speaking intellectually, in the day-light hard work doesn't seem quite as appealing. We forget what a good idea we once thought it was to do our warm-ups before every performance, to stay in shape between gigs, to do our research thoroughly, to memorize the right way, and completely.

That's why we need to rely upon discipline. And you do so. You do what you know you should do even when you've forgotten why you are doing it and a lesser man or woman would say, "I don't need to be a speaker, anyway. Just point me to the nearest potato chip!" That's why you have what it takes!

ACTING TIP:
SPEND SOME TIME WITH THE "PICTURE OF SUCCESS."

Technique #27:

TWELVE COMPONENTS OF A SUCCESSFUL
PERFORMANCE

Let's look at the fact that you have what it takes to deliver a successful performance from another angle, the angle of *the end*. From imagining—through imaginary *"hind-sight,"* if you will—let us pretend that you just made a fabulously successful presentation. Hooray! Now, what had to have happened—and must have happened—to make your speech so successful?

1. You felt you were in your right place. You were working within your niche or topic, you were at home in the venue, and you felt comfortable in your skin. You felt like an authority—you *were* an authority. You were right where you should have been, doing and saying exactly what you should have been doing and saying, and you were happy to be there.

2. You were clear and direct and engaging. You knew what you wanted to say, and you said it. And you addressed it effectively to your audience in that you involved them in the process. You made it a conversation.

3. You exercised good listening skills. In this conversation you listened to your audience as actively as your audience listened to you. You honored them. Even though you were more expert with regards to your topic, you realized you and they were equals in the world, and you welcomed their comments. And you and they both went away enriched.

4. You were open and accessible. You didn't hide behind a theory or doctrine. You gave what you had to give and you told the truth. And if you didn't know the answer, you told the truth about that, too, and because you had confidence in yourself and your

knowledge, you didn't feel embarrassed that you didn't know absolutely everything.

5. You were able to improvise and use humor. You knew enough—and were prepared enough—to come off of your "script" when something unexpected happened, or someone asked you an unexpected question. You used that occurrence as a gift—a "happy accident"—to further enliven your presentation. And you spiced it up with joy and humor, which endeared you to your audience and re-enforced their attention and support.

6. You maintained your credibility. Because you were knowledgeable, and well prepped, and honest and engaging and humble, and loved being there and loved your audience (are you getting the picture of what it takes?), people believed you. They believed *in* you. Then, all of a sudden, they had your back. And you knew it and you felt it, and it felt great!

7. You maintained your concentration. Working the way you have been working has helped you cement your awareness to the task at hand. These are the times when "time flies by." You and the creative task—whether it's speaking, writing, or cleaning out a closet—are one. There is no personality; there is no judge; there is no ego or fear. There is only the work, the activity. And you achieved this depth of concentration and commitment because you took the time to prepare. So you *knew* you were prepared. And you were willing to give what you prepared, and you loved giving it! Nothing could distract you from that.

8. You were entertaining, informative and inspiring. Your presentation was infused with your passion and excitement, and filled with useful content. And it spawned! It generated! Your speech sent its audience members out into the world enriched and motivated to add their contribution to the great community.

SPEAK *UP*! SPEAK *OUT*!

9. You remained confident and remembered the nobility of your purpose. You took care of us, your audience, but you also took care of *you*—which helped you take care of us. You kept yourself strong. You were aware of your value. And when it was over you weren't depleted; you felt renewed.

10. You answered tough questions gracefully. You didn't fight, you didn't argue, you didn't run and hide from confrontation. You loved. You loved the challenge and the challenger, and you stayed aligned with the truth as you saw it. You remained patient but you did not cave in to make "peace." When you couldn't find a resolution, you resolved to agree to disagree.

11. You hung in there till "curtain." Just the act of completing something, regardless of the quality of the final product, is occasion for celebration! Yay! You did it! And you did it well! Yes, there is always room for improvement, and we're always working on that. Fine. But getting to "The End" is big! And you did that. Congratulate yourself. You deserve it!

12. You handled stage-fright. You must have, at least to some degree, because here you still are! You're still with us! Hooray! You survived!

A NOTE:

Is that really good enough, though, to have just *survived* stage fright? I think we can agree that it isn't. It needs to be *handled*. So let's do that. Let's handle the last thing we need to deal with before we fly! Let's handle stage fright!

---

affirmation:

I am equal to whatever
is required of me.

146

SUMMARY OF MAIN POINTS

1. It is to the speaker's advantage to know how his scene partners—his audiences—are going to interact with him and respond during his performances. Find out as much as you can about your audience *before you ever step onto the stage.*
2. Love to perform! This will empower you with your audience.
3. Know that you have what it takes to be a good speaker. Review the qualities that are required, and own them!
4. Look at "The Twelve Components of a Successful Performance" from the perspective of hindsight, as if you have already made a fabulously successful presentation! This takes the pressure off and paves the way to perform naturally.

CHAPTER TEN

How to Handle Stage Fright

"Courage is being scared to death and saddling up anyway."
—John Wayne

WHY HANDLE STAGE FRIGHT? AND WHY NOW?

Because it's a bastard! Literally. Fear is an illegal occupant of the mind with no right to run rampant in our thinking. It needs to be seen as such and evicted! And why now, at this stage in our process, before we launch into the Techniques of performing, which finally takes us up onto the stage or up to the podium? Because I don't want stage fright to be there waiting for you when you get there! I don't want anything to stop your progress once you are rolling!

TAKING A TOUGHER STANCE WITH FEAR

I think we are all far too gentle with fear. Far too equal-opportunity in the emotions department. We tolerate it, *honor* it, even. Someone asks us why we did or didn't do this or that and we say, "Because I was afraid," and the inquirer backs right off and gives way with, "Oh, of course." Just like that, no questions asked. In the very face of what the masters of thought and thinking have been saying for eons: *"Don't be afraid,"* we cave right in.

Technique #28:
FACING YOUR FEAR/FACING YOUR LOVE

What are we afraid of? Everything: what might happen, what might not happen, that we've blown our chances, that we'll never get the chance. In a nutshell, that good is not real but evil is.

What are we afraid of with regards to speaking in public? Again, everything—speaking in public, we are told, is considered by most people to be one of the scariest activities any sane person can get himself into. Why? What's so terribly scary about it?

I've taken and given courses and workshops in acting and public speaking for over twenty years and in every session—whether I was taking it or giving it—the subject of fear arose, if not out loud, then at least prominently in somebody's mind, which an experienced teacher can spot a mile away. There's always a uniqueness to it—people are scared of different things; but there is also always a commonality. Let's look at that. Let's look at some of the most common reasons why people are afraid to get up and perform in public.

> ### *affirmation:*
> In every contest with fear,
> I have the upper hand.

WHAT SCARES YOU THE MOST ABOUT ACTING?

I asked one hundred actors, "What scares you the most about acting?" Here are the seven most common answers:

1. I won't be able to do it and I'll appear incompetent.
2. I'll go overboard and look like an idiot.
3. Mediocrity—I'll get by but never become a good actor.
4. The incessant waiting and rejection that goes along with it.
5. Dealing with the constant fear that I may not make it.
6. I'll freeze up and forget my lines.
7. I'll lose control and start to cry.

WHAT SCARES YOU THE MOST ABOUT SPEAKING IN PUBLIC?

I asked one hundred people in different walks of life,

"What scares you the most about speaking in public?" Here are the seven most common answers:

1. I just can't do it; I don't have the personal power it takes.
2. I'm not good enough or smart enough to take center stage.
3. I'll be boring; I won't be able to hold the audience's attention.
4. People won't like it (*me*.) They'll make fun of me.
5. I don't look good enough. (Out of shape, too heavy, etc.)
6. I'll lose my focus and then lose control.
7. I won't be able to manage my nerves.

If you had to condense and compare the answers to both questions, what would you say? Let's put this into an exercise.

EXERCISE:
"The Fear of Acting Compared
To The Fear of Public Speaking."

Condense the answers of the actors above. What, in a nutshell, are they most afraid of?

_____

_____

_____

Condense the answers of those responding about public speaking above. What, in a nutshell, are they most afraid of?

_____

_____

_____

Now compare them.
Which fears of each are most similar?

_____

_____

_____

Which fears of each are most different?

_____

_____

_____

ACTING TIP:
DON'T BE AFRAID TO BE FABULOUS!

WHAT APPEALS TO YOU THE MOST ABOUT ACTING?

I asked the group of actors another question: "What appeals to you the most about acting?" In other words, what makes it worth the risk, the uncertainty, the pain? What makes it worth the fear? *Is* it worth the fear? Why don't actors just give it up? And watch somebody else do it? Wouldn't that be more fun? Apparently not. Here are the actors' seven most common answers:

1. What appeals to me most is the feeling that I'm following my heart, doing what I want to do.
2. Being part of a creative endeavor with other interesting people.
3. "Being other people." I bring out things in myself that, otherwise, I wouldn't—including my dreams and aggressions.
4. Feeling fully present and completely spontaneous with something I rehearsed over and over.
5. The attention, the praise, and the money—plus the opportunities all that gives me.

6. The relationship with the audience—touching and inspiring them; making a difference in their lives.
7. Facing my fears and insecurities.

WHAT APPEALS TO YOU THE MOST ABOUT SPEAKING IN PUBLIC?

I asked the other group of people from different walks of life the similar question: "What appeals *to* you the most about speaking in public—if it does?" (It didn't to everyone!) Here are their six most common answers:
1. Feeling important and in my power.
2. The opportunity to express myself and shine!
3. It makes me be brave and conquer my fears.
4. The partnership and connection with an audience.
5. Feeling that I'm making a difference in people's lives.
6. All the love that flows my way.

Let's compare these answers as well.

EXERCISE:

"The Appeal of Acting Compared To
The Appeal of Public Speaking."

Condense the answers of the actors above. What, in a nutshell, most appeals to them about acting?

_____

_____

_____

Condense the answers of those responding about public speaking above. What, in a nutshell, most appeals to them about public speaking?

_____

_____

_____

Now compare them.
Which "likes" of each are most similar?

_____

_____

_____

Which "likes" of each are most different?

_____

_____

_____

A QUICK ANALYSIS

It doesn't take much analysis to determine that, in spite of the challenging fear that accompanies it—and it does, at times, seem formidable—those who act and/or speak in public find that the rewards of doing so more than compensate for the painful fear that seems to go with it. How wonderful it would be then—and how much better our presentations—if we could manage and mitigate that fear, so that we are left with a purer, less fear-filled experience!

Do you, too, love the feeling of following your heart, of working with other interesting people, the excitement of feeling fully present and spontaneous? Do you, also, love attention, appreciation, and money? Do you love being in partnership with an audience—touching and inspiring them with a sense of connection to something bigger than themselves—and making a difference in their lives? Do you love feeling brave and important and loved?

I can hear you answering, "Yes! Yes, of course!"

And I say, "Of course, you do!"

Then let us proceed! Let's enjoy more fully the wonderful bounty that speaking in public has to offer, and eighty-six that nasty demon—stage fright, in all its forms—that would keep us from doing so!

Technique #29:

RECOGNIZING STAGE FRIGHT WHEN YOU *FEEL* IT

Performance fear—*stage fright*. It doesn't need a sign on its forehead to announce and identify itself. No, it seems to move right in, uninvited, and take over your mind and body in the form of its unmistakable symptoms: *shaky knees, palpitating heart, churning stomach, tight throat, shortness of breath; a dark empty fuzziness in the head, a blank mind, the inability to focus your thought, stuttering; the inability to swallow, dry mouth, wet palms; a trembling voice, a nervous laugh.* Sound good? No? Well, these are some of the symptoms by which stage fright announces, "I'm home!" And it's going to stay home until you exercise your right to evict it!

"NERVES" CAN BE A GOOD THING, ACTUALLY

Like it or not, you can count on being a little bit "nervous" whenever you perform. It comes with the territory. You are getting up on stage, baring your soul and submitting yourself to judgment. I've never met a performer or speaker yet, in fact, who doesn't feel at least a little anxious when he or she gets up to perform. But that's not a bad thing. "Nerves" help you to lock your focus more sharply onto your work—*if* you don't let them run away with you and become full-fledged *stage fright*! That's the key. You can't completely rid yourself of all stage fright but you can manage it so that it remains merely "nerves."

ACTING TIP:
DON'T WAIT UNTIL THE FEAR GOES AWAY;
START AND THE FEAR WILL SUBSIDE.

So let's get down to it. What "causes" stage fright and what "cures" it?

Technique #30:

THE FOUR BIGGEST CAUSES OF STAGE FRIGHT

Why do we experience stage fright? We experience it because we want to be loved, approved of, and validated by others. We are standing, emotionally naked and exposed, in front of a group of strangers—or maybe not strangers—saying, in essence, "Here I am. This is what I have to offer," and we're not positive that even *we* think that what we are and have is enough. We know we're not supposed to care about what other people think of us and, God willing, eventually we'll develop enough faith in ourselves and in our work to override the need for "outside love." But right now we do care what others think of us, which makes us susceptible to stage fright.

> CAUSE #1: The first and greatest impetus to stage-fright is not having our motives and objectives in proper alignment. If we're up there on stage more for the purpose of being *thought* good than of *being* good; more for the money or other gain than to do a "world-enhancing" job; more to *get* glory than to "glorify" the truth in one form or another; then we're off our base and, naturally, we will be more likely to feel afraid.

> CAUSE #2: The second biggest—and the most "popular"—cause of stage-fright is not being prepared. Now, that shouldn't ever *have to be* a problem, because you shouldn't ever have to perform until you are ready to. You may choose, under pressure, to speak impromptu, but you don't *have* to do so. You can say no.

"So," you might ask, "if we don't have to speak until we are prepared, and we usually have time to get prepared, how can lack of preparation be such a big and common problem among speakers?"

I was hoping you'd ask me that! It's for the same reason that kids don't do their homework. They have the time, they just don't have the discipline to use the time on what it's meant for! Sounds stupid, right? That's because it is! And yet, we've all fallen prey to this stupidity. It's like we're back in high school. We have a geometry test tomorrow and we have an hour to study for the test tonight and we know that it will take that hour. But we decide to spend that hour talking to some guy on the phone who we know is only going to break our heart. Or we don't officially decide; we just keep talking and the time ticks by until it's too late, and we show up for the test in misery and we hate ourselves.

Fine, we've all done it. And you'd think we would have learned our lesson by now. But apparently not, because "being unprepared" still ranks as the most popular reason people become overwhelmed by stage fright! Are we gluttons for punishment, or does it just take a while to cop on to these things in this world? I didn't finally get hold of it till I was taking flying lessons in a single engine airplane, when being unprepared had severely more serious consequences!

It's not easy to do the right thing, even when it's a matter of life and death! We opt for the quick fix, to our eventual detriment. Why? Not a clue. What I do know, as your speech coach, is that if you don't take the time to thoroughly prepare, and you get up on stage knowing that you are not ready to perform, you are going to feel terrified up there. You are going to have stage fright, in a big way. And I don't want that for you! Even though it would be your own fault! (Which, of course, would be the tragedy of it.)

> CAUSE #3: The third biggest cause of stage fright is lack of commitment. This is a function of decisiveness, and fealty to your own sense of authority. If you are not fully committed to "speaking the speech," to being the mouth-piece, the vehicle —the matrix—for the ideas you are promoting, you are not going to feel stable and grounded in your created "reality." You are commanding the attention of your listeners when

you speak, and unless you feel your words are worthy of your command, you will waver in your sense of power and security, which equals stage fright.

CAUSE #4: The fourth greatest cause of stage fright is loss of concentration on the work at hand. If your concentration wanders you will become afraid. You will lose your place and forget what you were going to say, because you will have lost your anchor of truth, the thread within your own mind that would have kept you feeling secure.

Not having your motives and objectives in alignment, not being fully prepared, lack of commitment, and loss of concentration—these are the most common causes of stage-fright.

Technique #31:
THE SIX MOST POWERFUL CURES

One of the greatest lessons we can learn on this earth is not to indulge fear. I'm not talking about ignoring direction to get the heck out of Dodge when some danger is threatening you. I'm talking about the paralyzing anti-impetus that says something is wrong or is going to be wrong and there's nothing that you can do about it. Learn to recognize it. It first comes as a "passing" suggestion, a not yet quite fully formed thought. And that is the time to handle it. *"Nip it in the bud,"* as Barney Fife would say. Don't allow it to formulate—"to see what it will do"—out of curiosity. Then it's only harder to dismantle it because then it seems more real, although it isn't. But it seems so. Say, "No!" right away! Say, "No!" to the *negative* by embracing and practicing the *positive*.

We've discussed the four main causes of stage fright. Now, let's get to the important part— how do we dis-empower them? What are the cures?

CURE #1: Align your motives and objectives "ideally." (Clarity) Remember that you are present on stage or at the podium to do a job. Are the motives fueling the speech or presentation that you're giving in line with your motives and objectives as a *person*? Are the objectives stated throughout the speech itself consistent? Those are the ideals. Sometimes you have to "just do a job;" I understand that. But unless you act upon the intention to be "ideal" to the degree that you can, you never will be so. The good news is that, to the degree that you do, you will feel secure.

CURE #2: Prepare! (Certainty) We've been over this. It is obvious that we *should* prepare, and equally obvious that we *don't*! One thing is certain, dear Reader o' mine. If you want a fabulous work experience you've got to do a fabulous job. And to do that you've got to put the time into it that it requires. Love the prep as much as you love the performance. Because unless you do, you will not even love the performance!

CURE #3: Commit to the role. (Credibility) No matter what you do in life, your full commitment to doing it is the only way you are going to get others to believe that you can accomplish what you have set out to do. If you are running for president (of any group) but you are not fully behind being president yourself, you are not going to get supporters. If you are starting a small company but you're not thrilled about the products you are going to offer to the public, you are not going to secure stable investors. If you are expounding the "virtues" of certain policies to a group of executives around a conference table but you are not convinced that the policies are so very virtuous, don't be surprised if your executives don't buy that they are, either.

To make any headway with your speaking or presentation efforts—for others to believe in you—you *truly* do have to believe in yourself. Your passionate fealty to your own actions and intentions is the only means by which your words will command the respect and support of your audience. But when you have that support and the audience is with you, the camaraderie that emerges from that union embraces you so comfortingly that fear isn't even a question.

CURE #4: Practice. (Conviction) Practice, practice, practice! This is different from preparing. This is coming to know and imbibe thoroughly that which has emerged from your preparation and has formed itself into the body of your presentation. Once you have aligned your motives, prepared, and have committed to "the role," practice what has emerged into the form of your speech until you feel the conviction that "you've got it." To the degree of your conviction, you will feel less fear. Which is not to say that when you go up to perform you won't still feel butterflies; you will. But you won't feel that terrible doubt, the feeling that you are not ready. Practice until you feel the conviction that you *are!* Then, after you've done your relaxation and warm up exercises, go get 'em!

CURE #5: Concentrate. (Continuity) One of the greatest benefits of speaking in public is that doing so teaches you to concentrate. You have to concentrate, continue, remain, stay with it in anything in which you wish to succeed, but even more so when you are "on the hot seat" on stage or at the podium and have to remember and deliver a significant speech. It takes practice. It takes focus. Discipline your thinking to stay right in the moment and *on purpose*. This takes your attention away from yourself and into the spirit of service. And there is nothing so effective in dissolving fear as realizing that you are being of service to others.

CURE #6: Miscellaneous personal techniques or "tricks." (Comedy) This is where certain individual techniques, such as "imagine the audience naked" come into play. These ideas are meant to amuse and relax the speaker and level the playing field. And they can be helpful, depending on who is in the audience! Personally, I would find speaking to an audience of naked people quite unnerving! But, hey, different strokes! And that's the point—use whatever works for *you* to help eliminate insecurity and empower you. I don't know that that has to come at the expense of your audience, however, that you have to dis-empower them to come into power yourself. Better to bring them up, I think, than to knock them down. I heard a short (anonymous) poem years ago that has been of great help to me in this kind of situation and that I think might apply here:

> He drew a circle that shut me out—
> "Heretic, rebel, a thing to tout."
> But love and I had the wit to win—
> We drew a circle that brought him in.

In the long run, I think that the more life-affirming means of "curing" stage fright will better serve you.

A Short Re-Cap

The clarity of proper alignment of one's motives and objectives; the certainty that comes from thorough prepara-tion; the credibility that comes only from full commitment; the conviction that comes from enough practice; the sense of continuity that comes from devoted concentration; and a little comic relief when appropriate—along with the in-valuable skill of "vamping in place" when you forget your lines—combine, when practiced, to save you from the hor-rible torment of stage fright! These are your tools, and your *weapons*; learn to use them!

---

affirmation:

I am calm, ready
and willing, now.

Here is an exercise that—if you're game to try it—will be challenging but lots of fun, and very good for you!

EXERCISE:
   "Sing The Main Points of Your Speech."
List the main points of your speech. Note the natural progression of the points as your talk develops from premise to resolution.

FOR EXAMPLE: A presentation entitled, *"We Need to Re-Decorate Our Front Lobby."*
Main Points:
1. Premise: Our front lobby needs to be re-decorated.
2. The reasons why.
3. What happens if we don't do it.
4. The beneficial results if we do.
5. The costs.
6. Conclusion. (Re-state the premise.) Our front lobby needs to be re-decorated.

Now *sing* all of those points. That's right. (Think opera.) It's like you are speaking them but you are doing so as if in a song, underscoring each point with progressing emotion.

You will love this exercise, if you'll make yourself try it! It's great for busting inhibition, loosening you up, and for checking that the intellectual and emotional evolution of your speech is unfolding the way you would like it to. And it's fun!

Technique #32:
   HOW TO ANSWER TOUGH QUESTIONS

No matter how much you prepare for your presentations, every once in a while you run into someone whose purpose in life seems to be to give you a hard time. Here are a few ideas that may help you if you encounter a tough cookie in the audience.
1. Don't react.

2. Be sure that you heard what you thought you heard, correctly.
3. Ask the person to repeat what he said, or to put it a different way.
4. Give him the benefit of the doubt. (Try!)
5. Under-speak your answer, don't try to convert him or impress him with all you know.
6. If you don't know the answer to a question, say so; and offer to get back to her.
7. Don't apologize for not knowing something.
8. Tell him what you want ("Please bring this up in our Q&A at the end," for example).
9. Don't get tough unless you have to (you probably won't have to).
10. Bring out the arsenal: love and humor.
11. Refuse to be pressured into taking action until you feel inspired to do so.
12. Agree to postpone seeking resolution.

Sometimes, when people come at us aggressively, they are doing so because *they* are afraid. If you will keep your cool and don't attack back, they often relax and back down, because they feel safe now. We're all dealing with fear, learning how to handle it. It seems to be the biggest challenge in "the curriculum." Knowing that—that we're all going through it—gives us compassion for one another. And that compassion helps to lessen and disarm the "scariness" of others to us.

Stage fright, schmage fright! Nearly everybody in your audience is at least as scared as you are! I say "nearly everybody" because there are exceptions. Some people are truly actively working on mastering fear! Let's each be one of those people. Let's do that for one another.

SUMMARY OF MAIN POINTS

1. As a rule, we are far too lenient with *fear*!
2. Stage fright needs to be handled before we launch into performance.
3. Review what you fear and what you love about speaking, and resolve to magnify what you love!
4. "Nerves" are a good thing. But learn to recognize stage fright and disarm it.
5. The four biggest causes of stage fright are:
    a. Not having your motives and objectives aligned
    b. Not being prepared
    c. Lack of commitment
    d. Loss of concentration
6. The six most powerful cures of stage fright are:
    a. Aligning your motives and objectives
    b. Being prepared
    c. Commitment to "the role"
    d. Plenty of practice
    e. Concentration
    f. "Tricks" (miscellaneous personal techniques)
7. No matter how prepared you believe you are, expect tough questions.

CHAPTER ELEVEN

It's Showtime! #1:

Performance Techniques That Establish Your Authority

> "Nothing is at last sacred but the integrity of our own mind.
> Absolve you to yourself, and you shall have the suffrage of
> the world."
>
> — *Self Reliance* by Ralph Waldo Emerson

It's Showtime!

Finally! Here we are, ready to perform—all prepped and ready to go! Here are some techniques that will help you when you finally step onto "the stage." I've broken them down into two categories (and two chapters):

- Techniques that establish your authority
- Techniques that connect you with your audience

Let's begin with establishing your authority.

You Are Your Own Authority

Any time you enlist to perform a work of service, whether you volunteer or are assigned the task, to feel like you are truly being helpful you need to know that your effort is "authorized," backed by an "authority" that you respect. Who might that be, do you think? Ultimately, your authority to speak comes to you from yourself. Now, where *you* get it—from heaven or from the guy at the dry cleaners—is your own business. But as far as you and I and the rest of us on the world stage are concerned, you are the authority. And it is your ability to accept that fact—fueled by your desire to give—that "authorizes" you. It plugs you in and makes you feel like you are in your right place, doing your right work. And you are right.

It is this sense of authority that makes the speaker confident when she steps up to the mike; and feeling confident is fifty percent of the game, any game. We see this in sports, in politics, and in the many types of performance activities. But are there any acting techniques that can help support a speaker's feeling of authority when she is not exactly feeling it? Yes! Let's look at some of them.

Technique #33:

DRESSING FOR THE PART

When they dress for the part, proponents say, it helps them give themselves "permission to pretend." Then, in that freed childlike mental state, they begin to do the deeper work, the emotional work. Before that, though, they play.

Julie Harris, I am told, has always been a stickler for getting her costumes right before she begins to work on the interior life of her characters. The ways in which her characters and present themselves to the world (of the play) hold, she feels, invaluable secrets into their as-yet-to-be-created psyches.

You, the speaker, are also playing a role. You are playing the role of "a speaker." That much, we knew. The question is, what kind of speaker? You may be a mathematician speaking to a roomful of other mathematicians about new discoveries in the world of calculus. Fine. What do you wear? A wardrobe person dressing you for a film might put you in frayed corduroy pants long overdue for a washing, a wrinkled boxy suede jacket with lots of pockets, and a comfy, but not stylish, cloth cap of some sort. And you would give the impression that you were pre-occupied with your work and not in the least bit vain—physically, anyway. That impression would be rather cliché but, perhaps, that would be the impression the film director would choose to give.

And that's the point—intentionally or no, you are going to give an impression of yourself by the way that you dress "for the part." And, as many actors have discovered—and they are only *playing* it, while you are *being* it—the way one dresses has an impact, even on oneself! My suggestion to you, therefore, is that you cast this impression deliberately.

Does It Really Matter?

Does it really matter what you, the speaker, wear at the podium? After all, this is a speech, not a fashion show, and not a film.

Perhaps it shouldn't matter—like it shouldn't matter what others think about you—but, like it or not, the way you look plays a big part in making you credible to your audiences. And the way you dress and do your hair and make-up has a big impact on the way you look. William Hurt taught me this one.

For years, William Hurt has been another one of my heart-throbs. Out of the factory, he is blonde, blue-eyed, moderately buffed—a hunk often dressed in Ralph Lauren or Tommy Hilfiger. Adorable. But, suddenly, things had changed! I couldn't believe it! It was Bill Hurt, all right, but now—as I sat in the dark theatre staring at him on the big screen in *Kiss of The Spider Woman*—he was a skinny, weak, dirty prisoner dressed in filthy stripes, with acne, short curly red hair and glasses! *All of which was affected by wardrobe, hair and make-up!*

I learned the lesson well—wardrobe, hair and make-up, plus a little dieting, do, indeed, make a big difference in the way that you look. And again, the way that you look makes a big difference in the way you are perceived (and treated) by others. Now, if you don't like that—I don't particularly like it—you can add it to your list of causes and speak about it, if you care to. And maybe you can change it. In the meantime, though, you might want to be a bit more conscious about your fashion choices.

ACTING TIP:
DRESS THE WAY YOU WANT TO BE SEEN.

Guidelines for Dressing As "The Speaker"

Wardrobe

Dress "up." I don't mean wear a ball gown to a board meeting. I mean "dress for success." Dress as a successful person. Be the best dressed person in the style most appropriate for the occasion. If it is a group of business people that you will be addressing, wear, and tastefully accessorize, a beautiful business suit. If you are on board a large cruise ship, speaking about the wild life in Bora Bora, dress in well-made colorful cruise wear. You should be the best-dressed one in the room. Why? Because you and your ideas are the attention-deserving star of the moment! You are saying, "Look at and listen to me. I have something that you want." And if you don't look at least as put together and successful as they are, they are not going to buy that.

My acting students often ask me what they should wear to their auditions. Should they go "in costume"? If they are trying out for a cop should they rent a cop's uniform? I, generally, suggest that they dress simply, and add just a little flavor for the type of role. For instance, if you are auditioning to play a cop, dress as a policeman might dress when he's off-duty, then add a NYPD baseball cap. On the other hand, if you are auditioning to play a prostitute, don't show up in a Peter Pan collar. Suggest the image you want to register. These same principles apply to you as a speaker:

You might also consider wearing black or other dark colors, and avoid anything too loud in the way of a print. There are reasons why, in most headshots, actors wear black—almost everyone looks good in black, black is considered "dressy," so it meets the dress "up" rule, and black off-sets one's facial features, focusing our attention on the person's face. And keep your accessories to a minimum, so they don't distract your audience.

In short, look good. Disney's witch, Malificent, was ruthlessly evil, but she *looked* good! Lucille Ball, perpetual goofball that she was, was never without her make-up; she *looked* good. Dress the part you are playing—the SUCCESSFUL SPEAKER—and look as good as you can.

HAIR AND MAKE UP

Hair and make-up come more into play with actors. To speakers I say, keep it simple. Use "hair" and "make-up" for enhancement but don't do anything to take your audience's attention away from your message.

Technique #34:
USING YOUR BODY LANGUAGE

In Chapter Seven we talked about developing effective body language during, and for, rehearsal. Now let's talk about its role in performance. We know that, through our gesturing and other physical behavior, we are continually displaying to others what we are thinking. The challenge in performance is to control your body language so that you reveal only what, and as much as, and only when, you want to. This keeps the way you are behaving within your control and in service to your message. What does this body language consist of, and how can you use it most effectively in your performances? It consists of the following:

1. Your hands. *"What do you do with your hands?"* people often ask me. The question is largely euphemistic. It implies nervousness and lack of self-control. "What do I do with my*self* when I'm nervous and feel all thumbs?!" they mean to say. But that needn't be the case. On the contrary—"What do you do with your hands?" You speak with them. You punctuate your points with them. You point. You guide. You pound your fist into your palm, you hold up your fingers to count, you turn your palms up or put them together and bow your head. You *use* them! What you do *not* do is put your hands in your pockets, or scratch yourself, or wring them nervously. You let go and allow your hands and body to gesture normally. And they will do so if you will trust yourself and not interfere with their natural contribution to your communication. Let's play a moment.

EXERCISE:

"Exaggerate Your Gesturing."
Here is a piece from our sample text.

Our Sample Text Piece #3: *"SNOW WHITE"*

"As Snow White grew, she became more and more beautiful, and by the time she was seven years old she was as beautiful as the day and more beautiful than the queen herself. One day when the queen said to her mirror: "Mirror, Mirror, here I stand. Who is the fairest in the land?"—the mirror replied: "You, O Queen, are the fairest here, but Snow White is a thousand times more fair."

The queen gasped, and turned yellow and green with envy. Every time she laid eyes on Snow White after that she hated her so much that her heart turned over in her bosom. Envy and pride grew like weeds in her heart, until she knew no peace by day or night."

Memorize a portion of the above text—then deliver it aloud using extremely exaggerated hand and body gestures.

Like so many acting and public speaking exercises, this exercise is meant and great for busting inhibition. But it has an even greater value for you. When you try it, you realize that some of the gesturing that you thought would be so "over the top" wasn't really over the top at all! It was, and is, perfectly appropriate! And now you can adopt and incorporate it into your speech-giving without any embarrassment or self-consciousness.

2. Walk, carriage and posture. The way an individual walks, carries himself, and stands says a lot about him, or her. It reveals information about his culture, his socio-economic condition, his sense of self-esteem, the degree of comfort and/or fear he feels in his world, and the way he feels physically that day. Like with clothes, hair style and makeup, these things must be "put on" his character by the

actor. Do you remember Dustin Hoffman's crouched posture and shaky walk in *Midnight Cowboy*? Katharine Hepburn's unquestionably upper crust, entitled carriage and posture in *The Philadelphia Story*? Or the classic: Charles Laughton's posture in, and as, *The Hunchback of Notre Dame*? Your steady walk, your firm carriage, and your erect posture are important elements of your character as "the successful speaker."

3. Mannerisms and staying in control. Are you aware of the signals you are sending when you are in the presence of another person? Are you aware that you drum your fingers or stir your teacup with the rapidity of a woodpecker's beak when you are nervous? Or that every time Bill walks into the room you cross your legs? Everyone has good and not-as-good mannerisms and habits—tell-tale body language—that define them. You might take this into consideration and modify your behavior to the end that you are sending only the signals you want sent.

4. "Business." Often when creating his character, an actor (or his director) gives his character a bit of "business." And that's just what it is, busy-ness, some action—usually a small one—that gives the actor something to do that, defining his character, keeps him grounded. A well-known example of this is the actor Benecio Del Toro in the film, *The Usual Suspects*. Del Toro saw his character as both nervous and desirous of maintaining control, and he wanted to give him some "business" to illustrate this. Do you remember what he did? He gave him a Chapstick that, with one hand and without looking at it, he used his thumb to continually flick the top off and on again. As part of his prep, he practiced for hours until flicking the top off and on his Chapstick had become second nature.

171

Here's a twist: as speakers, we often want to do the opposite. We work to minimize any extra activity that would draw the audience's attention away from our message. The point, either way, is *control*.

> 5. Eye contact. Some speech coaches will tell you to look over your audience's heads and address the rear wall. These people are cousins to the "imagine them naked" set. It's fear. They're afraid to touch, to connect, to become influenced—all of which, when you are feeling "in your power" and in your love, you not only don't resist but welcome.

In Lillian Hellman's play, *The Little Foxes*, a young woman is about to take a rather long train trip by herself. Her mother and aunt, wishing to protect her, tell her to keep to herself and not to talk to anyone. Her boyfriend arrives just in time to say farewell and, after a quick kiss goodbye, calls after her to reach out and talk to as many new people as she can! (And we see why she loves him!)

Make eye contact with your audience; make *contact* with them. Make your event a conversation, a happening. You needn't worry that you'll lose control. *Don't lose it.* Keep the reigns in your own two hands, even while you are allowing others to pet the horses. And when you have finished allowing someone in your audience to participate in some way, just say, "That's good. That's enough. Thank you. We're moving on now." And do so.

> 6. Smile. What a powerful mood-controller a smile is! It controls the energy in a room more efficiently than an air conditioner controls the temperature. Nobody's safe! You smile at somebody and they're a goner. Even if they don't show it by smiling back. Which is their prerogative. But it's your prerogative to smile at your audience. And things will go much more to your, and their, liking if you do.

7. Staying visible "at the helm." All "dressed up" with . . . no one to see you? What good is that?! "Let's go downstairs and let Mrs. Trumble get a load of us!" Ethel Mertz said to Lucy Ricardo when they had graduated from "charm school" and were, she thought, dressed to the nines. In theatre, there's little value in a character's even existing if he cannot be seen and heard. What this means for you, the speaker, is that you need to be not only seen and heard, but seen as the person in charge, the captain of the ship. And you do that—in your own way—by acting "big!"

Technique #35:

ACT *BIG*!

I began teaching acting on my own in 1991. Before that, I occasionally taught Lorrie Hull's children's class as a substitute teacher. Lorrie (Loraine S. Hull) was Lee Strasberg's senior faculty member at Strasberg's Institute in Los Angeles for twelve years. She wrote the book, *Strasberg's Method*. She was one of my acting teachers, a wonderful teacher, and is still teaching as I write this. I also taught kids as a sub for Al Pacino's private acting coach, Ed DeLeo. Then I went on my own in 1991. I emptied my living room and taught out of my home in Hermosa Beach, California for a couple of months, then, as enrollment quickly grew, taught at the Hermosa Beach Kiwanis Club. The Club owned a wonderful single standing building on the edge of a park right around the corner from my house. I rented the building for my classes—two evenings a week for adults, and Saturday mornings for kids. In addition to the classes, I offered my students something else at no additional charge: I produced and directed a monthly half-hour public-access television show I called "Act *BIG!*" The format went like this: I opened the show with a short introduction as to what the theme of that particular show was; then three scenes were performed by my students; then I closed the show with a short wrap up

173

and thanks. The show ran several times each month on local television stations in thirty-one cities in the Los Angeles area, giving my students some well-appreciated (and well-deserved) exposure. Everyone seemed to love the name of the show: "Act *BIG!*" because they loved the concept. We all have a choice. We can play or act small in our lives or we can act big. What's it going to be for you, as a speaker?

I think we get confused at times. We get mixed messages. We're told, "Get out there and grab the bull by the horns and make something of yourself!" But we're also told, "don't be too big for your britches," and to be humble. Hopefully, you have sorted a lot of this out by now—the conundrums and paradoxes of life; you may even be speaking about such things. For our purposes here, though, let me be clear as your coach. You are more effectively communicative on stage or at the podium—as well as more humble—when you act "big" than when you act "small." And here's why—we're back to the idea of the "shrink-wrapped person."

Have you ever seen a singer who was extremely restricted in her body language when she was performing? I have. (I've *been* that singer!) She didn't sway to the music, or tap her foot, or snap her fingers; she just stood there like a board as she sang, making the audience feel thoroughly uncomfortable. She would have done us all a huge favor if she would have loosened up, gotten into the groove and *moved*. Taking her cue, we would have relaxed, gotten in her groove and moved with her. Would she have been egocentric and self-important and vain by tripping the light fandango a tad? Or would she, in fact, have been more generous by doing so, providing us with a more satisfying experience? That's right, door number two. But she was scared.

When you are performing a speech, you can stay behind the podium, be very still, offer no arm movement or hand gestures, and speak just loud enough to prevent some self-appointed spokesman for your audience from yelling out, "*We can't hear you!*" Or, you can do your job! You can voice the message that you or someone else has employed you to voice by communicating fully, unambiguously, and clearly.

Not because you have a big ego but because you have a big job to do! And a big heart with which to do it.

So, *you* tell *me*. Are you being too big for your britches when you are "acting big?" Or are you being loving, because effective? Are you being more "self-less" when you play small? Or are you really being more self-*ish* because you are separating yourself from others? I always think it's better to go a little bigger and let someone (a director, for instance) suggest that you "take it down a bit," than have people thinking, "Can you, please, give us a little something here?!" Remember, when we are focusing on ourselves we always think we are being bigger than others see us.

EXERCISE:

"Exaggerate Your Emotions." Repeat the "Exaggerate Your Gesturing" exercise above, only this time also extremely exaggerate your emotions.

Technique #36:
CLAIMING THE STAGE AS YOUR OWN

A speaker usually gets less time "on stage" prior to his performance than an actor does but he can usually manage to get *some*. And I highly recommend that you do so. Not to get familiar with "the set"—which, for a speaker, usually consists of little more than a board room, or conference room, or auditorium, filled with empty chairs and a podium. But more as a claim of rights and authority. Your claim is, "This place is my place and *I am the one!*" And you have been given the authority. This is huge for the speaker. You are actively empowering yourself.

"This is my place. Mine. No one else's. I am the one whose task it is to give this talk today. In all the universe, 'the great speakers' bureau in the sky' has selected me to do this work. And this place is my venue. I am the commencement speaker at Yale next week. Or, I am closing Wellness Week at Vassar tomorrow night (which I have done). Or, this room behind the meat counter at The Piggly-Wiggly Market in Van Nuys, California, where I have been asked to speak in about twenty minutes to nine butchers about teamwork, is my stage. I am on assignment, an assignment that I take very seriously."

Whether you "claim the stage" days before you speak or you are able to "stake your claim" for the first and only time as you ascend the steps of a stage in an already packed and pulsing house, you can still take a moment to accept—with humility and self-respect—that this occurrence and your part in it are sanctioned by the same intelligence that sanctions everything else good that is going on that day or evening in our universe. Step up to it. Step up to the plate. Then wave to your audience, blow them a kiss, and do one hell of a job for them!

---

affirmation:

No one is luckier than I am.

Technique #37:

GRABBING THEIR ATTENTION
ON THE DOWNBEAT

In a mystery play, the playwright sometimes chooses to open the play with a crime, *to start off with a bang*, so to speak. Some speakers start off with a joke. Some ask an intriguing question to engage their listeners in an intellectual pursuit. Here are a few sample grabbers you might try:

- a joke or short story
- a song
- a news item you picked up on the way to the venue
- a challenging question
- a shocking statistic
- a simple stunt or bit of business akin to a magic trick
- or just a simple introduction to a well-structured talk that lays out for your audience what they may expect

What are these speakers and writers who employ these grabbers doing? They are grabbing the attention of their audience the very first second they get a chance to! This can be tremendously exciting for an audience. Like a confident lover, the speaker who relishes his ability to control the experience of his audience for the purpose of benefitting and pleasing them is well appreciated, provided he can deliver on his promise! This is not a bad thing, not a bad sense of "control;" this is a performance, after all. And the speaker has the best chance of getting and maintaining that control if he gets it at the downbeat and never lets it go.

Technique #38:

SELLING YOUR MESSAGE, NOT YOURSELF

The surest way to keep yourself in line with your inspiration and to do a good job is to start out—and remind yourself continually —that you are here to sell your message, not yourself. This doesn't take away from your authority, it secures it. You are on assignment. You have "papers." You are "in the system." You have something important to say. But it's not about you; it's about the message. Except that it sort of *is* about you, in that you are the one saying it, and that, without you, it might not get said. But it's still about the message.

Technique #39:

BEING IN THE MOMENT

"Being in the moment" is the name of a classic acting exercise used in acting classes all over the world. It is one of the most effective ways of helping an actor, a speaker, or anyone (and that is its value) to calm, center, and concentrate his thinking. It functions as a sort of psychic wormhole (if I've got that right). Or a vacuum cleaner hose. It sucks or gathers your actions, your thoughts, your plans, bringing them all right into the present moment, and yells, "Stop everything you are doing and start all over, right now! Be right here, in this place, at this moment." This trains the actor to keep his concentration on his work, not only so that he doesn't forget his lines, but so that he can also go, uninterruptedly, deeply into his characterization. In the Zen philosophy this technique is called "present mindedness" or "mindfulness." We all know how good it feels when the self dissolves into some task and the hours fly by. Learning to be in the moment is a soul-satisfying skill for everyone.

To you, the speaker, the ability to "be in the moment" is invaluable. It concentrates your attention and power on the task at hand. It reinforces your confidence that this is the one and only place for you and your audience to be at this moment. Being in the moment is the only way you will ever have the most fulfilling experience that speaking in public can afford you—the realization that you and the truth are one.

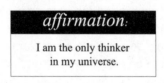

affirmation:

I am the only thinker
in my universe.

Technique #40:
MAINTAINING YOUR CREDIBILITY

The credibility factor. The thing that makes you believe in yourself, your audience believe in you and your message, and that keeps the audience staying and coming back for more. The truth, the rock; the judgment made by each of us that makes it "a go!" What is it based on, this vote of confidence that cannot be bought? Your credibility will be judged on the following:

- Your depth of personal knowledge and experience.
- Your level of preparedness.
- Your enthusiasm during your presentation performance.
- Your appearance.
- Your language.

- Your body language.
- Your practice of doing what you say you will do.

Let's look at these:

1. Your depth of personal knowledge and experience. Even more than the depth of a speaker's knowledge, the depth of her personal experience is what counts with her audience. Do you speak as the pundits and the punks do, who just want to hear their own voices? Or does your speaking touch the heart? For you to be credible, your audience needs to know, to feel, to be convinced, that the knowledge you are expounding is not only true but has touched you and affected you in some way. It doesn't have to be really heavy, such as: "Let us stop war!" But it does have to be genuine, such as: "Tracy needs you all to get measured for your company softball uniforms by Thursday or she won't have enough time to make them." We, the audience, want to know that you believe in what you are talking about at least enough to be truly behind it.

2. Your level of preparedness. We've spoken about preparation, especially with regards to research and rehearsal. But looking at it from the standpoint of the speaker's credibility, how prepared does a speaker need to be to be credible?

This is a sticky point with me (on behalf of my students and clients) because it misleads them. And it was something of a trick question to you.

I'd really like you to get this, so please listen up. Prep doesn't have a level. There is no *level of preparedness*; you are either prepared or you're not!

Take an actor. He's learning a role. He has to memorize his lines. Time's running out. He knows he should spend time on it but he puts it off another day. Then he spends a little time on it. He sort of gets it. He thinks, hopes, *gambles,* that he's prepared *enough*. But he isn't. He performs and he falls short. What a surprise. And he's miserable, which is exactly what he deserves. And yet, he was a victim! He'd bought into the mesmeric suggestion that he could get "sort of prepared," so he didn't get prepared at all.

Or a speaker, an executive, whose career rests upon the presentation she's about to make to her company's board and shareholders. She has the main points in her mind and she thinks she'll be able to wing the rest. She thinks she's prepared *enough*, because she has some good ideas, and she's a hot shot.

"WAKE UP!" I want to say to these people. "What is the matter with you?! No, you may not go to the movies with your sweetheart. No, you may not go to that dinner party. YOU HAVE TO PREPARE!" I mean, *what the hell?!*

> 3. Your enthusiasm during your presentation performance. It is when you are prepared that you can be the most enthusiastic in your delivery. Because then you're free! Once you've got your lines—your speech—down pat, you can play! You can pause between lines; you can add lines between lines; you can interject a joke if it occurs to you. Because you know where you are and where you are going, you are secure. You inspire even yourself! And this makes you enthusiastic, which encourages your audience to believe in you and what you are saying.

> 4. Your appearance. We've spoken a lot about appearance and about how much of a part it plays in helping you to define yourself to your audience. When "who you are" and "who you appear to be" are one and the same, this increases your credibility with your audience.

> 5. Your language. The language that you use and the way that you use it. Language is provocative. The trick is to be sure that it provokes as you wish it to.

In acting we learn that language—the words—are secondary to the emotions they are meant to convey; that words are, in fact, carriers of the emotions. First we have a feeling: You feel love for Bob and you want to tell him that you love him. Well, you're in luck! A long time ago—over a long period of time—some amazing people agreed that making certain vocal noises would represent the fact that you love Bob, the caveman. In fact, different groups of people from different areas agreed on different groups of sounds to represent this fact; these constitute the various languages. But we do all agree that if you want Bob to know that you love him, you are a long way ahead in getting your point across to him if you use one of the groups of sounds that we've agreed mean "I love you," instead of one that means "You look like a toad."

Which boils down to *right use*. Use the right words in your speeches, will you? Use nice, beautiful words. And pretty language tricks like alliteration and rhyming and rhythm . And be clear—not vague, not confusing—in your meaning. And use your cuss words sparingly, with the precision of a poet. Skillfully communicating your feelings and information to your audience in line with your intentions will increase their confidence that you are credible because it will be clear to them that, at least, you know what you are saying.

ACTING TIP:
SPEAK ELOQUENTLY.

6. Your body language._ Just as your words express your emotions, so, too, do your actions. As we have discussed, you gesture naturally. Your posture reflects your mental stance, naturally. Your facial expressions mirror your beliefs and opinions. If you are angry your body will show it. If you feel annoyed, or afraid, or very happy, those emotions will register on your face and body. This happens naturally because the mind and the body work together. You

are always projecting what you are feeling to others. Your credibility with your audience will increase to the degree that your language and your body language concur.

7. Your practice of doing what you say you will do. The last measure by which your credibility will be judged is—*Do you do what you say you are going to do*? If you tell someone in HR (human resources) that you will get back to them about your schedule by Thursday, do you get back to them by Thursday? I don't have to tell you this. Just know that people do keep score. And while they may give you *one*, they won't give you *two*. I think it helps if you promise people as little as possible, then deliver *more*. Don't say, "I'll call you Tuesday;" just call Tuesday. And if you do make a promise, jot it down and then deliver on it. Because nothing damages credibility so quickly as false promises and hypocrisy.

SUMMARY OF MAIN POINTS

1. Ultimately, the speaker, like the actor does, receives her authority to speak from herself.
2. To help him- or herself "get into character," the speaker dresses for "the part" of a speaker.
3. The way the speaker presents himself makes a powerful impact on his audience.
4. Whatever your message is, your body language plays a large part in its being successfully delivered to your audience. Learn to control your body language.
5. Act Big! Make your emotions and physical gestures large and easily readable.
6. Claim the stage as your own, and that you have the right to be there.
7. Grab your audience's attention on the downbeat!
8. Sell your message, not yourself.
9. Maintain your credibility.

CHAPTER TWELVE

It's Showtime! #2:
Performance Techniques That Connect
You With Your Audience

"The communication with an audience—it's a communication that goes beyond religion, beyond politics. It goes to the core of each person. It has to do with a universal humanity."

—F. Murray Abraham

REMIND YOURSELF WHO YOU ARE!

We've all seen bumper stickers that serve to remind us to appreciate others, such as, "Have you hugged your child today?" But have you reminded yourself lately how truly terrific you are and how lucky your audiences are to have you address them?

I see this—*or the lack thereof*—with actors all the time. They go on an audition, for free, after having spent hours prepping, dressing, traveling, waiting—all for free—and then they show the casting director, director, producer, whomever, their interpretation—their *professional* interpretation—of what it would be like if they got the part. Then they, the actors, say, "Thank you, thank you!" and want to write thank you notes "for giving me the opportunity to…" blah blah blah! I suggest to them that they remember just who did the giving, here. Yes, they were "given the opportunity," and, yes, they did it by agreement. But *they* did it. I suggest that they keep still until someone on the other side of the table says "thank you" to them, and that they then, graciously, but with self-respect, answer "You're welcome." Then they can add, "Thank you, too," if they can't help themselves!

I say the same thing to you, the speaker. "God's gift to men? To women?" You betcha! To both! And you need to know it. After having established your authority and right to be speaking at an event, realizing your value in the lives of your audience is the most important thing you need to do in order to connect with them because that establishes and keeps the relationship in its proper perspective.

Technique #41:
REALIZING THAT THE CAST IS
ALL IN IT TOGETHER

At the beginning of a theatrical production, once a play has been cast the director will call for a table reading. The cast members assemble around a large table in a theatre or a rehearsal space, each with a script before him or her, and read the play from start to finish. When they come to a point of conflict, and one character says, "You took Suzie and all my money, darn it!" and another says, "Tough!" the actors don't push their chairs back from the table and take it outside! They know that they are in this reading together, and have a common purpose. Even when they perform the play on stage a few weeks later in costumes in a more real-seeming environment, they still know that the conflict going on between the characters they are playing is not going on between *them*. On the contrary, they are of one mind, one purpose, undivided; not in conflict at all. For the common purpose of serving the truth in the play, they are *pretending* that they are apart. But In fact, "the cast is all in it together."

Whenever a speaker—a political activist, say—steps up to the podium, an attorney stands before the jury, a sales person lays out her proposal, or a club member takes the microphone to make an announcement, he or she has the same opportunity that an actor has to claim that this event is that of a partnership. It is a group commitment, that of a company, and that speaker and his audience are in it together. They are all aboard the same ship—of which the speaker is

Cap-i-tan—and they all want the same thing—a safe journey brought to a safe and satisfying conclusion.

---

affirmation:

I am complete.
I do not need anything
anyone else has to offer me.

LOVE THEM

"Oh no!" you say. "First I had to love to perform, and now I have to love *them*?!"

One day, years ago, I was about to step into a business meeting. I was producing television commercials at the time and the two men I was about to meet with were clients of mine. I was going to tell them that the extras they wanted (over and above what my company had agreed to do for them within our initial budget) was going to cost them more money. I was nervous—I was younger and they had more experience than I had. I sat by myself for a few minutes, trying to get some clarity. It dawned on me: we wanted the same thing. We were in business *together* on this project and so, to succeed, we had to want the same thing.

At first, that didn't seem true. It seemed just the opposite, in fact. But the idea felt so comforting that I stayed with it though I had no idea how it would play out. All I knew—all I'd seen—all I was going to stay with was that we were on the same team. They were no longer my enemies. I was no longer afraid of them.

I joined them in the conference room. I felt love for them—not forced, but brotherly love. After all, we were in it together, on the same side. They asked me how much the overages would cost. I told them. They approved them. We shook hands and that was that.

Now, if I had tried to cheat them, or they had tried to cheat me, things wouldn't have resolved so easily. But as it turned out, we did want the same thing: a well-produced commercial at a fair price, so there was no real conflict. The only problem was the fear that the other would be less than honorable. Which was superseded by the realization that we were "all in it together."

The speaker's partner—*your* partner, your fellow "cast member," the one with whom you will be engaging in a common venture and who wants the same thing that you do—is his, your, audience. You need them; without them there is no performance. You are in partnership with them. Together, you and they will be creating and experiencing the production that is your presentation.

Technique #42:

SPEAKING *WITH* THEM, NOT *AT* THEM

And need I add: never *down* to them? Nor up to them, for that matter. "As in life," (our standard) address whomever you are speaking with as equals. This makes for a much nicer day, of course. But more than that, the goal is to *engage* your audience. So that, even though you may be doing 95% of the talking, the perception in the room is that you and they are having a conversation. When you converse with your audience you are not just throwing words and concepts at them; you are discussing, analyzing, holding it all up for their consideration. You are speaking *with* them.

KEEPING CONTROL OF THE ROOM

Most audience members will respect the speaker and abide by her boundaries. But once in a while you encounter a frustrated performer. You know the type. He wants the attention and glory and he thinks that the best way to get it is to discredit the one "whose right it is." Be ready for that, and cut the little blood-sucker off at *the root*. You can do it with humor, or with some all-purpose "We'll deal with that later" phrase, but don't give it air to breathe. (We talked about how to answer tough questions in Chapter Ten.)

You know who is great at this? Judge Judy (Judith Sheindlin). I'm serious. Have you ever seen her show? She's a little slip of a woman and she takes absolutely zero guff. If she's not talking to you and you pipe up, she will knock you dead by your second syllable. She will tap her pen hard on her wooden desk and tell you in a raised officious voice to "Be quiet!" or "Don't talk!" Or "Unclasp your arms!" "Put your hand down!" "Sit down!" And they do it. Big, muscular, scary looking men who could snap her like a twig do exactly what Judge Judy tells them. Of course, they *are* on television, and they are in court, and she does have an armed bailiff beside her. But still. She takes her authority seriously and she knows that she has to keep control of her courtroom.

You have to keep control of your room as well. If you wish to engage with your audience in the spirit of a little more give and take than Judge Judy does with her plaintiffs and defendants, however, here are a few suggestions that might help you.

HOW TO ENGAGE WITH YOUR AUDIENCE

1. Look at them! You would be surprised how many speakers never really look at the people who make up their audience! The speaker has been told, as I've mentioned, to look over the tops of their heads and address his remarks to the rear wall of the room. So that everyone in the room will have heard the address but no one will actually *have been addressed*!

I think speakers who work this way do so because they are afraid that if they truly *see* somebody that means that somebody will truly see them. But I, as your coach, want you to *want* to be seen. I want others to "get you" on a level deeper than just words and ideas. I also want you to empower others to give what *they* have to give.

2. Smile! Embrace your audience in your warm and loving smile. We are yours for a short time, and it is in your power to teach us, to inspire us, to help us. How generous of you to make the contribution that you do. Good for you. And good for us!

3. Put all the chairs in a circle. This depends upon the size of your audience, the venue, and the nature of your topic. But if you have a small crowd, fewer than twenty, say, and the venue and your topic will allow for it, you can create a relaxed, friendly atmosphere by putting your chairs in a circle. If your audience is larger, find another way to effect a haven of friendly intimacy.

4. Laugh! All the world loves to laugh! Laughter frees us from fear. It reminds us how good life really is. If anyone can get out of here having deserved the epitaph, "He made people laugh!" I'd say that he had done all right. Wouldn't you?

In Chapter Eight I included heavy bouts of forced laughter as one of my vocal warm up exercises prior to presentation. This is because it is physically impossible to laugh and hold on to tension at the same time. If you can make your audience laugh a good, hard, cosmic laugh, because you are genuinely laughing yourself, your audience will love you! And they will participate in the communication with you in whatever ways you lead them to.

> **ACTING TIP:**
> MAKE, AND KEEP, EYE CONTACT.

Technique #43:
MEANING WHAT YOU SAY AND SAYING IT THE
WAY YOU MEAN IT

MEAN WHAT YOU SAY . . .

When I'm rehearsing an actor for a role, I often find myself calling out to her after she has delivered some line that I didn't believe she meant, "Mean it! Don't just say it; *mean* it." Because unless the actor truly means what she is saying, her words won't mean anything to her audience. It is the same for the speaker. The speech-writer, like a playwright, may have put the meaning into the construction of the speech, but it won't come off the page until and unless that meaning is delivered by the speaker.

For example: I can recite The Pledge of Allegiance. You can, too, possibly. "OK, let's race!" And off we go! One of us wins. So what? Did it have any meaning? Did we mean what we said? Not at all. We just recited words. Grotesquely, obscenely, we rushed through something of great importance and gave it no importance at all. Bad speaker! But if I said, "Let's do it again—*you* do it—and *mean* it this time," how might it go?

"I pledge allegiance," you would begin. Only this time you would make a commitment with the very first word—"I." Not someone else, not a group, no one but you. But you *do*. You do what? "I pledge . . ." Does that mean that you have decided, so definitely that you now give your word? "I *pledge* . . ." Pledge what? "I pledge *allegiance* . . . And so on. It takes time and commitment on your part to work this way. But unless you do, unless you *mean* every word that you say, you will not be believable to your audience.

. . . SAY IT THE WAY YOU MEAN IT

If we know what we mean, what could possibly keep us from saying it the way that we mean it, you might ask? Well, a variety of things: lack of concentration, insecurity, a change of heart, disruptions in the auditorium. But unless you can cut through all of that and say what you mean *the way that you mean it*, you will not be communicating with your audience.

AND SAY IT IN AN INTERESTING WAY!

This is actually a request. So we don't get bored. And we have a little fun in life. Spend a little time considering how you might say what you have to say in a more interesting and exciting way. Please! Let go! Spice your point up a bit—with humor, a story on yourself, a story on someone else—with his permission. We want to get your message but we'd also like to have a little fun along the way. We'd like to be informed *and* enlightened. We'd also like to be made to laugh. As my second favorite movie star—Daffy Duck (right after Cary Grant) says, "It *is* to laugh!"

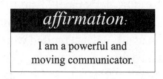

affirmation:

I am a powerful and
moving communicator.

Technique #44:

PLAYING YOUR PART WITH FULL EMOTIONAL ENUNCIATION

A speaker's emotions and opinions and points of view need to be clearly discernible by the audience. We, the audience, don't want any subtle what-is-she-feeling ambiguity. If an actor is meant to be feeling angry, we want to see, clearly, that he is angry. If he is meant to be feeling delighted, let us be clear that he is delighted. Don't leave us in doubt or uncertainty. We want to be able to read what the actor is feeling. And we want the same clear emotional read of our speakers.

If I ask you to enunciate your words, I am asking you to say them with precision, to the end that I might more clearly interpret their meaning. When I ask the actor or speaker to enunciate his emotions, I am asking him to feel them more precisely, to the same end—that they communicate, or transmit, meaning more clearly to me. Don't make your audience guess! Define what you think and feel, and display that for your audience to comprehend.

Unlike the actor, though, the speaker is not taking a point of view that is one among others; he—you—*are* the point of view up on stage, the only one. So it is very important to the success of your presentation that the audience gets the correct impressions from you. And that will only happen if you are "playing your part with full emotional enunciation!"

Speakers are not neutral. Society may have tried to make you neutral, to restrict you, to hinder you. It may have told you to be quiet, to not make waves or draw attention to yourself or to disturb the established, reigning order. But that doesn't work with the public speaker. And it didn't work with you! That's because, often, it is, in fact, the very function of the public speaker *to* make noise, *to* make waves, and *to* draw attention to his ideas; to intentionally disturb the established reigning order if, in his view, it warrants disturbance and reform. And you have always known that. There is no fence-sitting in drama, and there is no fence-sitting in public speaking. The speaker knows what he has to say and he says it with full emotional enunciation.

Don't Be Afraid to Wow! Them

I always tell my students and clients before their performances and presentations to be fabulous! Be bold! Be wonderful! You can be, you know; it's your natural state. And being so is more of a service to us—with more "role model" value—than saying, "Excuse me for living, I'll hurry up and get off the stage and hand it over to someone else more deserving." Besides—to *whom*? Who are you going to hand it over to that's better or more deserving than you are? No such person exists. *You* are the one. It's your turn, your time. So, wow us! The ones who understand this will applaud and support you. The ones who don't will learn from you.

Technique #45:
USING THE PERSUASIVE POWER OF HONEST EMOTION

Laughter is contagious, especially the OMG, grab your sides kind of laughter. Or the cosmic giggles. Or the highly inappropriate *"uncontrollables,"* like when something strikes you and your brother funny at Aunt Minnie's funeral. So, too, are honest tears contagious. We feel for and *with* one another when the emotion is deep and true. That's one of the main reasons we go to the theatre and watch films—to be moved. We want to laugh and cry, and we are moved to do so by the persuasive power of honest emotion.

This is useful information to the public speaker. It is not only license for you to feel your feelings deeply and fully at the podium, it is a demand that you do so. Because your doing so is crucial to persuading your audience to accept what you are offering them.

This is one of the places where, when I tell people that I am an acting coach, a sales person might chime in and say, "Yeah, I *act* all the time." He means he has to put on a false face and pretend—with *dis*-honest emotion—that he likes the product or point of view he is selling, that he cares whether or not his potential buyers will benefit by his product, and that the price his company has set is fair. In other words, when the salesperson says he acts all the time, he means that he lies. But that's not what acting is. That's not what public speaking is. That's not what good salesmanship is, either. These dishonest portrayals of emotions and beliefs are the exact opposite of using the power of real emotion honestly.

NOT EVERYONE IS A CYNIC

Truly. Not everybody in this world is a cynic. Far from it. Most people really do want to be, and to do, good in the world. You, as a public speaker, are a prime example of someone who comes across certain ideas she finds valuable and wants to share with others. Are you to be considered insincere because you endeavor to persuade your fellows to accept what you are offering them? For me, when you believe that what you are offering is good for people it's perfectly OK to be persuasive. But never are you "acting" when you sell. When you sell, you are either extending an offer of help to your customer, or you are lying to them.

If, on the other hand, you *don't* try to convince your audience of the value of your ideas, what are you even doing there? You'd *better* persuade your audience to, at least, consider what you are bringing to them or you are wasting your time! And the best way to persuade them is to have wonderfu ideas that honestly move you. Nothing less would even get their attention.

ACTING TIP:
SPEAK YOUR TRUTH SHAMELESSLY!

Technique #46:

LISTEN!

There is nothing that establishes communication between people so effectively as their ability to actively listen to one another. To listen to another person, without feeling like you have to jump in and register *your* thoughts, *your* feelings—even to "help" him in any way—is an act of mature, intelligent generosity. Most people can't do it. They feel they have to *participate*, failing to realize how tremendously valuable a good listener's contribution is to any conversation. A good listener is a sounding board against which an individual can try out his or her ideas and then make *his own* conclusions, via the authority of his own mind, as to their value. A listener's *just being there* can encourage an individual to speak out when, otherwise, he might have remained silent, and facilitate the participation of someone who may be speaking for the first time. And that is pretty special.

But in the world of public speaking, in which the speaker does all the talking, there's no one that he needs to listen to, except during Q&A, right? No, that is wrong. As we have established, even if the speaker "does all the talking," every good speech is a conversation. There is a lot going on mentally in the room, and the speaker who is a good listener can hear that, and he responds to it. It leads him to "now make *this* point" or "better skip *that* one," and the speaker attends to this guidance.

Good listening on the part of the performer is one of the things that make performing *live* so exciting! Good, deep listening is an extremely intimate act. Like a good lover, you are reading your "partner" with skillful sensitivity, modifying your performance as called for. If anyone ever tells you that you are a good listener, take it as the high compliment that it is. Listening is as important to the public speaker as the speaking itself. Let's reduce this to a formula, shall we? *Speaking + Listening = Speaking.* Good!

THE SPEAKER IS THE RESPONSIBLE PARTY

Who—you or your audience—is responsible for the successful transmission of your ideas to them, do you think? Right! *You* are! You, the speaker, the leader, the reader, the spokesperson, the one at the podium, at the head of the room, on the stage. The one commanding the big bucks, or, at least, worthy of them! The one we are all here to hear. You are the one responsible for the success of the two-way communication.

If you have a present for me, say a book, whose responsibility is it—yours or mine—that I get it? Do I get wind of the potential gift and grab it out of your hands? Or is the transfer of the book into my possession part of what defines it as a gift? It's simply a book, isn't it—not a gift—until you have successfully transferred it into my hands. Likewise, the public speaker is responsible for the successful delivery of his gift, his message, into the hearts and minds of his audience. And the sooner you accept that responsibility as the speaker, the sooner you will step into your power and make it happen.

Technique #47:
   USING COMMUNICATION CONNECTORS

Somebody taught me this and I've found it most useful in communicating ever since. It's this: Check in with the occasional "Uh-huh." Don't leave the person you're talking to hanging out there on the line all by himself when it is so easily in your power to ground him. He says something, you don't respond; he's not sure if you heard him or if you heard him but disagree with him, or *what*?!

You've felt this, right? You make some pithy comment about the politics in Borneo and your "scene partner" either says nothing at all or says something totally unrelated, like, "Too bad Starbucks doesn't make that rich hot chocolate anymore." And you're thinking, *"What's up?!"*—that she was just waiting for you to shut up so she could say something. And you feel completely unsatisfied. She certainly didn't put the gift of making you feel understood and secure in your hands, did she?

Well, when the shoe's on the other foot and it's in your hands to be the generous listener and caring communicator— here's what you can do. At least, here's how my friend taught me when he said, "Kathryn, I would appreciate it if, when we are talking, you would check in with the occasional 'Uh-huh.'" It works like this:

Every once in a while, as you are listening to your communication partner speaking, throw in one of the following "connectors" to help keep the communication connected: *Right; Yes, that makes sense; Oh, yeah, I see your point; I understand; I see; I hear that; Uh-huh.* Even, once in a while, when you think it is warranted, go so far as to mirror their point back to them, something like this: *So what you are saying is . . .* and then restate their point in your own words.

The effect of this practice is tremendous! The one speaking to you feels *heard (*which is *the* main reason he will think you are a good listener, by the way) and, more important, the practice will keep you both on the same page, truly communicating. I mean, it always worked well for my Great Aunt Constance and me. OK, maybe our use of it (*my* use of it) was a little bit different.

Aunt Constance was a good woman but as time went by and she hit her nineties she grew a little negative when it came to how she saw her fellow man, as well as increasingly vociferous about it. She couldn't quite get her fill. She'd tell you (those one or two of us who would still call and listen to her) what one SOB or another had done or said to her that day, and then she'd tell you again, rarely letting you get a word in edgewise. So, to keep my sanity, as well as my relationship with Aunt Constance aloft—which I maintained mostly for my Dad who had loved her before he passed on and she became so audibly angry—I employed the invaluable "communication connector," which, fortunately, I had learned by that time. During my fifteen or so minutes of, well, you can't exactly call it "conversation" with Aunt Constance, I would lay the telephone receiver down on my desk and go about my business—a little straightening here, a little filing there—and then, every two or three minutes, I'd pick it up and say, "Uh-huh," or "Oh, dear;" even, every once in a while, "Geez, that's terrible!" to which she would invariably respond—because it fit every time— "It sure is!" and then I'd lay it back down again. And by the time is was over, Aunt Constance would feel (somewhat) heard and that we'd had a nice visit, and my brain hadn't turned to mush. Plus, I got my filing done.

Using communication connectors with your audience members (during Q and A, for instance) helps you stay connected to them by making them feel heard by you, which makes them love you, which makes them more likely to embrace your message.

CONGRATULATIONS!

You made it through your presentation performance! Way to go! High five! Does that mean you're done? No. Is there more to do? Yes. But what an achievement! What a mile stone. Congratulations!

SUMMARY OF MAIN POINTS

1. After having established your authority as a speaker, realizing your value in the lives of your audience is the most important thing you need to know in order to connect with them.
2. Realize that "the cast" is all in it together. Your speech is a group effort; make it a win-win.
3. Speak *with* them, not at them. And never down to them.
4. To engage your audience, look at them, smile at them, create a haven of intimacy, and laugh!
5. Mean what you say and say it the way you mean it. And make sure that you say it in an interesting way!
6. Play your part with full emotional enunciation. The speaker's emotions, opinions and points of view need to be clearly discernible by the audience. After all, your intention is to communicate to them! And don't be afraid to *wow* them!
7. Use the persuasive power of your honest emotion. Go ahead—*sell it*, if you believe in it.
8. Cultivate the art of good listening. Good, deep listening is an extremely intimate act.
9. Ultimately, it is the speaker who is responsible for the successful transmission of his ideas to his audience.

"It doesn't matter how big the acting is, how loud your roaring. It must never be absolutely at the top of your range Always leave something in the reserve tank."

— Laurence Olivier

Technique #48:
KNOWING WHEN NOT TO SPEAK

Sometimes our power and our influence lay in our saying less—if anything at all. Don't speak in the middle of an "ah-hah" moment, for example—that *you* orchestrated, when it is obvious that the audience is getting your point and you see their entire lives changing before your eyes. At that point, be quiet! Let it happen! Do not add another "insightful" comment. Let "the spirit" take over and forge the connection or solidify the point in the minds of your audience. This is part of your gift to them. If you keep talking you will oversell your audience. You will frustrate them. And anger them. And fail them.

EXERCISE:
"Gratitude A." List three things you are especially grateful for. (Don't over-think this.)

1._____

2._____

3._____

THE LESS SAID, THE MORE POWERFUL THAT WHICH IS

A few years back, I took a vow of silence for a month. I allowed myself to laugh aloud, but that was it. I uttered no other sounds.

The first couple of days it was torture. I felt like there was so much that I needed to say. I needed to comment, I needed to advise, I needed to compliment—not to mention to excuse and to justify! But I couldn't, so I didn't, and the world went on! The logistics of it were that I told my mom and a few friends about it beforehand, I left a message on my answering machine saying that I would be reachable only by mail for that month, and I kept pen and paper on me at all times—on the top sheet of which I had written, "I've taken a vow of silence for a month but I can write." And I carried on with my life. I even drove to my insurance agent's office and negotiated new car insurance with him, with just pad and pen on my part.

After the first couple of days, I began to love it! I loved the way I felt and I loved what I was learning. Here are some of the things I learned.

1. Not everything has to be said.
2. We always communicate from a place deeper than our words.
3. It was a relief to not have to weigh in and comment on everything!
4. I realized that not only I but most people talk more than necessary.
5. The silence served as a wall of protection to me from the prying thoughts of others.
6. I saw the things I would have said if I hadn't promised to keep quiet—for the thoughts formed; I just didn't transmit them—and I was often glad that I hadn't. I saw how fear-based many of them were.
7. Retaining even my more "profound" thoughts didn't seem to deprive the world *at all!* On the other hand, I was present and I was thinking my thoughts, and communication was going on between others and me mentally. Plus, I had pen and paper, so it wasn't

like I was exactly superfluous to life. But much of what I generally said, I learned, was.

8. I felt more relaxed.
9. I dealt with my own mind and thoughts—even when in company—more than with what was going on external to me.
10. Not everything has to be said. (But some of it should be said more than once.)

EXERCISE:

"Gratitude B." List three *more* things you are especially grateful for.

1._____

2._____

3._____

---

affirmation:

I am secure, successful and satisfied.

Technique #49:

DESTROYING DESTRUCTIVE CONVERSATION

There is a conscious effort going on now among writers and public speakers of all genres on several continents around the world to be more precise and specific in their statements and to refuse to fall into the sophomoric, hyperbolic tendency to use generalizing or polarizing language. For instance: "All (fill in the blank) people do (fill in the blank) all the time." This kind of blanket thinking is narrow and leads to bigotry. It's something to watch out for. Here are some things you can do to help eliminate polarizing.

1. If you hear someone make a sweeping generalization, you might ask them to cite some specifics. Poor Sarah Palin is a good example: "I read *all* of them (opinion-influencing political magazines.)" And yet, she couldn't cite even one of them. In *your* work, be specific. It lends to your credibility.

2. Use language that brings people together, not the "us and them" language that keeps people in separate clubs. Celebrate our unity in diversity. Gathered together, we make one great big colorful bunch! Each one of us, individually, is also multicolored.

3. Court diversity, not corroboration. "Be broadminded." And tolerant, and patient, with yourself and others. Don't seek to destroy (*ruin the structure of),* the views or opinions of others. Have a conversation on a topic that is important to you with a person who thinks very differently from you in general and on this topic in particular and seek only to understand and be understood. Do not try to persuade them to change their mind and adopt your view.

4. Support and stand up for people who are under attack for expressing a different view.

ACTING TIP:
DESTROY DESTRUCTIVE INNER
MONOLOGUES ABOUT YOURSELF.

SAY IT ONCE . . .

Say it . . . *and then hush up! Please!* We'll give you a dollar! Just, please, don't tell us over and over again six ways to Sunday what you already said. I'm not talking about repeating a statement for emphasis—that may be called for. And, yes, you want to make sure we got it—that your beloved got her "gift." But once you've transferred it safely into her hands, you don't need to make her swear that she got it, ask her for a receipt for it, and then make her have the receipt notarized!

And don't be long winded. The fact is, it looks better on you if your audience knows they have to pay attention to you because you have more important things to do than repeat yourself and go on and on, than if they're fidgeting in their seats because they are bored.

Technique #50:
　　USE HUMOR—OR HUMOR WILL USE *YOU*!

Humor is right up there with the best of the great cosmic weapons: love, honesty, and courage. Very popular, humor is. Everybody loves humor. Humor could run for Sheriff of the great cosmic mind, and win. Sheriff Humor would never let your thinking get too out of line. He would temper things with a little . . . humor. He would step in when someone who had the floor was taking himself too seriously, and everyone— audience and speaker—would relax again.

The fact is, as big "big-kids" as we try to be, we can only take so much seriousness. Comic Relief exists as a character in the cosmic cast for a reason: we need occasional—and regular— breaks! As a speaker, you need to know this and to give us those breaks. Because, if you don't, we, your audience, will break OUT and take them ourselves, at your expense, if necessary.

Like with Sister Mary Matilda. Fourth grade (ours, not hers.) We drove her over the edge. Literally. Good-bye St. Bridget of Sweden grammar school, hello loony bin. We didn't mean to but we couldn't help it; she had no sense of humor. It was her or us. I felt bad—I *was* bad, and so were some of the other girls. But the boys were ruthless. They did all the bad stuff we've so come to depend on fourth grade little boys to do, and they did it in spades! *Thank goodness!* They *saved* us from a fourth grade without humor! One morning we came to school and were simply informed by Mother Mary Paul that Sister Mary Maltida had "gone away." But we knew. We got a sub, Mrs. White, who was a holy terror, far meaner than Sister Mary Matilda ever was. She hit us with rulers and kicked our feet if they were sticking out from under our desk when she was passing by. But at least Mrs. White enjoyed herself.

HUMOR IS A MINDSET

Real humor is not restricted to the occasional joke in speaking; it is a mindset, an approach that seasons your entire performance, no matter how serious the topic is. The mindset is that, "while life is not always easy, it is filled with meaning and irony, and so much that is beautiful, that, in spite of much testimony to the contrary, we may trust it."

EXERCISE:

"The Three Part Humor Exercise."

a. Notate something you witnessed lately that you thought was funny.

_____

_____

_____

b. List ten jokes you know.

1. _____

2. _____

3. _____

4. _____

5. _____

6. _____

7. _____

8. _____

9. _____

10. _____

c. Now, tell one or more of your jokes to three people. If they laugh, keep the joke in your repertoire; if not, cut it! And keep your ears open for new jokes. Good, *smart*, jokes are a delightful addition to any conversation, or speech. And (a lesson from Sister Mary Matilda) having a couple of funny jokes up your sleeve might just keep you out of the loony bin.

Technique #51:
  STAYING IN CONTROL UNTIL "CURTAIN!"

It isn't over until it's over (and it's not even over then!) But it is definitely not over until it is. And sometimes, when it seems it's as good as over—because we are having a bad moment, or a bad performance—something will often happen at the last moment that saves the day!

This happens in races, doesn't it? The racer has a bad start. It seems like he might as well just leave the track and come out again another day. But the racer is a professional and he behaves like one. He amps his effort and hangs in there. And occasionally, at the last minute the energy shifts and one of the other racers falters and our hero or heroine wins the race!

This happens for actors as well, often for the betterment of the play! The actor has a crummy start—she's not "in the moment," she loses her place. But, somehow, those very foibles rouse her—anger her, even—and she fuels her final monologue with extra passion that thrills the audience like never before!

For you, the speaker, this may mean—when you forget your place in your speech—that you *use* that to dig deeper. Perhaps you recall and deliver a pertinent story from your past. What you do *not* do, *ever*, is throw in the towel, give up, cave in, or apologize. You do not say, "Sorry, I'm not very good at this," or "I'm nervous," any more than a carpenter would say, "I'm sorry," when he drops his hammer. To the best of your ability, pick it back up, re-set your focus, control your attitude and mood, remind yourself of your objectives and goals, monitor your body language, and carry on until you have finished your assignment. If you are asked tough questions along the way, answer them to the best of your ability. (See Chapter Ten for tips.) But hang in there! You are staying in control until "curtain!"

EXERCISE:

"Gratitude C." List three *more* things you are especially grateful for. Make these big ones.

1. _____

2. _____

3. _____

Technique #52:

LEAVING THEM WANTING MORE

Laurence Olivier said, in essence, never let them see the borders of your range. Don't play it full out. Don't strain for your highest note. Leave yourself some wiggle room. There should be an element of safe comfort that you maintain throughout the delivery of your speech. Don't let the audience feel that you are working too hard. Or that you are giving them too much. Do not let them think that you are giving them all that you have to give. On the contrary, as with a new sweetheart, you want your audience to feel like they are getting just a taste of what you have to offer. *Oh, you have so much more you could give! If you felt like giving it. If the stakes warranted it. You were pleased to give what you did, though; pleased to share, only too pleased. Got to go now, though. Got to go be fabulous somewhere else now!*

You make all this work, and make them want *more* of it, by virtue of the fact that it's true! You *have* merely scratched the surface of your understanding and expertise, and all around fabulosity!

ACTING TIP:
BE HAPPY TO GIVE BUT DON'T GIVE EVERYTHING.

Technique #53:

ALWAYS TAKE YOUR BOW

Don't be shy or hesitant about taking your bow. It gives your audience the opportunity to thank you for what you've done for them. It also allows you to thank your audience for the opportunity to be of service to them. And don't be in a rush to get the applause over with and get off the stage, either. Enjoy your moment. Actors know this. You don't see them rushing off the stage and giving their moment to someone else, do you? No. And neither should you. Enjoy the love. You've earned it. It's yours, and it feels great!

EXERCISE:

"Bows." Practice taking your bow. Try different bows, with different head, arm and hand positions. Find two or three that feel the most comfortable to you.

affirmation:
It's great to be alive!

SUMMARY OF MAIN POINTS

1. It is as important to know when *not* to speak as it is to know when to speak.
2. Let your message, not *you*, do the talking.
3. The less said, the more powerful that which is said.
4. Not everything has to be said.
5. Destroy, and refuse to be party to, destructive conversation.
6. Use humor on a regular basis, or humor will use you!
7. Stay in control until "curtain."
8. Leave them wanting more!
9. Always take your bow. It gives your audience the opportunity to thank you.

"To become a great and successful speaker, the thing you must do is practice. You have to speak and speak. I had some forty-five years in show business . . . but I never really started living to my capacity and fulfilling my ability until I became a full-time speaker."

— Art Linkletter

NOW *WHAT?!*

What do you do after you have delivered your speech? And the last of your admirers has shaken your hand and is walking away. And the maintenance man steps inside and waits by the light switch for you to gather your belongings so he can close up the venue for the night?

Maybe you'll meet up for a drink with some friends or colleagues; maybe you'll go straight home. But sooner or later you will go home. And when you get there you will think about your performance, hopefully with a big happy grin on your face!

Technique #54:
ASSESSING YOUR PERFORMANCE

Here is a check list to help you evaluate your performance in a constructive manner. I've based it on the two lists in Chapter Nine: *"Knowing That You Have What It Takes,"* a list of qualities and skills that make you a great speaker, and *"Twelve Components of a Successful Performance,"* which is just that.

YOUR PERFORMANCE EVALUATION SHEET

1   Did you do your warm up exericses before you performed?

_____

2   Did you feel you were in your right place, and happy to be there?

_____

3   Grade your confidence level (1-5; 5 being highest). Grade your relaxation level.

_____

4   Did you smile?

_____

5   Did you make and keep eye contact?

_____

6   Grade the organization of your material and your explanation of your main points.

_____

7   Were you open and accessbile to your audience?

_____

8   Did you exercise good listening skills?

_____

9   Were you able to improvise and use humor?

_____

10 Did you learn anything? What?

_____

11 Did you "hang in there till curtain?"

_____

12 Grade your posture, carriage and standing.

_____

13 Did you keep your concentration? What, If anything, threw you?

_____

14 Were you entertaining, informing and inspiring? Were you passionate?

_____

15 Did you answer tough questions gracefully?

_____

16 Grade your appearance: wardrobe, hair, and make-up.

_____

17 Did you handle stage fright?

_____

18 Did you take your bow?

_____

19 Did you remember the nobility of your purpose?

_____

Did you do a good job? Of course, you did! Congratulate yourself. Then, in the next day or two, make notes as to where you were strong and where you wish to improve, make your follow up calls—to cap this speech, gather your "reviews," and book future speeches—and then move on.

Technique #55:

SECURING YOUR ENCORES AND REVIEWS

A musician is rewarded for his crowd-pleasing performance by his audience's prolonged applause, ceasing only upon his reappearance on stage and immersion into another number. The actor responds to the adulation of his audience by answering multiple curtain calls, bowing more deeply to his audience each time. The speaker is rewarded for her good performance by strong applause, followed—if the speaker will allow it—by the formation of a line of audience members who want to speak one-on-one with her for a moment.

This is the speaker's encore. It's an opportunity for both parties to spend a few minutes with one another individually. It helps you get to know your audience. I'm not suggesting that you give them your phone number or offer them a ride home but a moment of respectful contact in a public place in which you allow your audience members to thank you personally, ask you a question, or shake your hand, is considered quite common between a speaker and her audience and can be quite satisfying to her. As always, though, do only what makes you comfortable.

Gather Ye Your Reviews While Ye May

We all know how valuable it is to an actor when The New York Times gives, for example, his work a good review. Business goes, *up*! The same phenomenon holds true for the public speaker. Therefore, gather your precious reviews!

For a speaker, these "reviews" come in the form of recommendation letters from the organizations or individuals who engaged you. Did you speak about "wellness in the workplace" for Citicorp.? Then ask the head of Human Resources who booked you to give you a review: a glowing letter of recommendation to other firms and organizations. Did you speak on "ending hunger in America" for The United Way, and did it go over well? Good! Then, ASAP, ask the individual who booked you to write a short paragraph describing—with just the right amount of hyperbole—how absolutely wonderful you and your talk were.

THE TRICK TO GETTING GREAT REVIEWS

Would that it were that simple! But you can't just ask for letters of recommendation—which you deserve and that are so useful in helping you get future business—and expect to get them. You have to *get* them! And that's not easy. People are busy. Besides, they're done with you now. You came, you delivered, and they paid you. And now you're bugging them for a letter of recommendation? It's not that they have qualms about recommending you, you understand. But to have to *write* something, about someone who's no longer even on their agenda! And their resistance only worsens with time. Which is why you need to get the letters as soon after you've spoken as you can!

Well, here's what you do. You help them. How? You write the recommendation letters for them!

This sounds rather presumptuous, doesn't it? It is! But it is also a brilliant solution. You save people who are busy—and may not be that comfortable with writing to begin with—time and effort; and, two, in composing your own letter you emphasize the points that you think will do you the most good in securing your future work. In other words, you control the composition. (The person you are writing it for doesn't have to sign it if he or she doesn't want to!) And—you get your letter in hand!

Handle it like this. After you've tried two or three times by phone and email to get the person to write you your short recommendation letter that he promised he would—and now he's not even taking your calls—get this message through to him somehow: "Tell Bob I know he's busy but, as I'm sure he knows, these letters are very important to me. So how would it be if I drafted the letter for him and he could then just put it on his letterhead? And, of course, he could change anything he wanted to."

Personally, I've never had this fail. And you get the most glowing recommendation letters this way! peaking of which—don't be reserved. If you do go this route be good to yourself—don't be too modest. Let this letter do its job for you. After all, it will only be telling the truth—you *are* fabulous—and it will help encourage others who will benefit by your presentations to give you a chance to come speak to them.

---

affirmation:

My success is
presently occurring.

Technique #56:

A SPEAKER IS A SPEAKER EVERY DAY

The fact that you scored well in your event does not mean that "you're done;" it only preps you for the next one. We are proud of you—don't misunderstand me. But never succumb to the temptation to sit back and coast. Why would you want to? The joy and the power of life are in the living and the giving of the life that you are, not in laying back. That's not to say that "rest" and "pleasure cruises" shouldn't be regular items on your agenda; they should be. But stay connected. Like with a diet—factor in "dessert on Sunday" or a piece of Mary Lou and Tad's wedding cake, but don't say on Sunday, "I'm off my diet." We all know where that leads. On the other hand, don't work too hard. You know how hard you should work. Work only that hard. Anything more will prove inefficient, and make you unhappy, and we don't want that. And keep growing as an individual, so you continually have interesting things to speak to us about.

ACTING TIP:
KEEP A JOURNAL OF ANECDOTES,
STORIES AND JOKES.

REGARDING THE "OFF-TIME," THOUGH?

How, though, can the speaker best use his "off-time?" Here are a few things you can do between engagements to continually grow as a public speaker.

1. Eat a good breakfast, take out the trash, and say your prayers. Take care of yourself, on a daily basis. Take in a few nourishing ideas, download the garbage (it will start to smell and attract vermin if you leave it too long), and center yourself in preparation for the day. Speaking is something you *do*. Your daily life is what you *are*—and your contribution in the form of your art will come from that. So take care of yourself first. And don't think that you are an exception and can skip the basics, because you are not. (Which, actually, can be very comforting when you apply it to such facts as "everyone is talented and entitled to success," *and you are no exception!*)

2. Do your exercises. Practice your cold reading. This is such an important skill to have, and you develop it in private. Do your relaxation and vocal warm up exercises for *concentration* and *projection*. And remain playful and imaginative.

3. Read the masters. For an actor, that means read the writings of the master acting teachers, such as Stanislavski, Lee Strasberg, Uta Hagen, Sanford Meisner, Robert Lewis, Michael Chekhov, Stella Adler, S. Loraine Hull, and whoever else strikes his fancy, as well as the master playwrights. Read plays! Loads of them, aloud.

You, the speaker, will find it very helpful, and fun, to read the monologues from the great plays aloud. Feel the words in your mouth. Find the musicality in the delivery. Invite a few friends to come over to read a play as a whole. Read aloud speeches given by master speakers working today—the inspirational and motivational speakers and politicians—as well as speeches by the great orators such as Lincoln, Franklin, Kennedy, and King. This challenging, and fun, training will stand you in good stead when you are again standing at the podium.

4. Study with several teachers and coaches. I recommend this for speakers as well as for actors. Working with a knowledgeable and sensitive coach to help you develop your own style as a speaker will do wonders toward increasing your confidence—and *castability*—as a performer.

5. Talk with other speakers. Find out how they do it. Share info to learn how others work, who they study with, how they prepare. Be philosophical, experimental and creative. We are all on the same team!

6. Attend the talks and workshops of other speakers. Especially if they are speaking on your topic(s). See and hear what else is being said and expressed out in the field. This will help you customize your presentation more in line with your unique take on the topic, so that you bring something to the party that others do not.

7. Keep a journal. Insights come like small white butterflies that flit quickly away. Be prepared to capture them. One may be the spirit of a whole new topic for you.

8. Get involved in the work of other speakers. Actors do this all the time. Between gigs they visit the theatres and sets their friends are working in and on, and offer to help out. As a speaker, you can tag along on your friend's speaking engagement, take the money at the door, collect business cards, take notes, handle the mike during Q&A, or just be his pal. Doing this keeps you humble, keeps you learning, and keeps you active in this multi-faceted world of ours!

9. Do your spiritual work daily. This is our most important daily practice. It opens our vision and helps us recognize opportunities to speak when they present themselves.

10. Be adventurous. hink about giving a seminar or workshop. Sponsor it yourself. We love leaders who provide opportunities for others. Be one of those leaders. The point is: keep developing and growing whether you are on the platform, on the stage, at the podium, in the conference room, in the school room or any place else on this fabulous planet. Stay active. Go to a museum, or a

movie, or the park. Make lunch for someone you would enjoy having a nice conversation with. Read. Search. Write. Accept that you are never really "between gigs." Like an actor, the gig of being a speaker is an on-going continuous adventure and her time away from the podium merely constitutes a different phase of it.

ACTING TIP:
TAKE VERY GOOD CARE OF YOURSELF.

EXERCISE:
"Three Things You Agree to Do."

List three things that you agree to do for your speaking career this week. Be sure that you mean it; you are making a commitment.

1._____

2._____

3._____

Now schedule them. And make sure that you do them!

AFFIRMATION: I am continually being led to my right audiences.

Technique #57:
REMEMBERING THAT SPEAKING IS A SERVICE JOB

Somebody told me once that if you want to give a good speech, all you have to do is just stand up and say what you're grateful for. She said character is more important than technique, so if you are sincere in your gratitude, that will prove "technique" enough. The heart trumps the head every time.

How wonderful—and how grateful we are for it—that we have the ability to stand up in front of a group of our fellow beings with the vision and the drive, *and the courage*, to hold the room rapt while we speak on a subject that we feel is important. People often say they want to make a difference in the world. Being a public speaker is a great way to do that. You can change people's lives. Your ideas and your words can change the world.

There is no call to get all nervous and excited before you step out onto the stage or up to the podium, however; because, like acting, public speaking is really a service job. You've got a job to do, that's all. But what an important job it is! With the truth that it is your job to tell, you are enlightening minds, comforting hearts and freeing souls. You are being paid the highest compliment when an organization invites you to come speak to them. Cherish it!

Technique #58:

ALWAYS PERFORM WHEN ASKED

In addition to being *willing* to perform whenever asked, you have to be *ready*. What this means for an actor is that he has a current "audition packet" in his pocket. It might include three monologues (one dramatic, one comedic, one classical), two songs, and a poem—enough to choose from that would be suitable for any audition opportunity. But what does it mean for the speaker? Can the idea of the audition packet be of use to you? You are not called upon to audition for making a speech the same way that an actor is for a part. Nevertheless, I have found that if a speaker has his own performance packet, consisting, perhaps, of pieces of two marvelous speeches and a couple of poems—which he keeps sharply on-call to his mind—he feels more prepared to perform when asked than otherwise. He has something ready to recite if called upon.

Try it. And throw in a song, for good measure! Even if you don't think you can sing. Lots of actors and speakers "don't sing," but I make them do it anyway. And often they are the ones whose performances break your heart.

BE READY

How many times were you asked to recite, or sing, or play an instrument, but fear, inhibition, or insecurity prevented you, largely because you weren't ready? They make for sad stories, those wounded moments of being unprepared, don't they? Don't let it happen again. Opportunities don't keep regular business hours. Get prepared for your next opportunity and maybe next time you won't turn it down.

Technique #59:
ASSERTING YOURSELF (SOME MORE)

I spoke about this in Chapter Five, but it's so important I thought I'd *assert myself* and talk about it a little more! Don't be afraid to assert yourself! Life is such that we often have to "get up and go get it ourselves." And that's all right. "Breaks" come, but usually not in big sizes. So don't wait for them. Cultivate self-assertion. You may be called a bit pushy but people will admire you for it, and add, "I guess that's what it takes to get it done." And they will be right.

EXERCISE:
"Six Places Where You Would Like To Speak."

List six places or venues or groups of people where or in which or to whom you would like to speak.

1._____ 4._____

2._____ 5._____

3._____ 6._____

Consider speaking there, or for them, as very real possibilities.

Technique #60:

REMEMBERING THE NOBILITY OF YOUR PURPOSE

You have the right to know that you are contributing to society through your work. Make the decision that you are willing and want to work, then opportunities will start falling from the trees they do so opulently grow on. Earn your success by putting in the time necessary to do a good job. Don't rush. Don't take shortcuts. By being thorough you will discover what your niche *in the play* is. Find that. Be that. Be willing to do that work, and you will find that you will *have* work, because you will be speaking from your unique authenticity, which is a crucial part of the overall cosmic puzzle. You are becoming involved in a life-long process in this work and you need never feel pressured to get it all done in a moment. Get in the groove, like the birds and the bees—chirping and buzzing happily away; and enjoy the process of being and growing, and of speaking *up* and speaking *out* about it!

Another thing: don't worry. You are ready to take your next step. You have all the talent and courage of the ages residing within every cell of your being. You are the best there has ever been. You are a present from God to us. We are grateful for you. And we can't wait to see what you are going to do next!

affirmation:

Life is good.

SUMMARY OF MAIN POINTS

1. Congratulate yourself on the completion of your performance!
2. Assess your performance.
3. Secure your "reviews" (letters of endorsement and recommendation) as soon as you can.
4. Keep yourself sharp between speaking engagements.
5. Remember that speaking is a service job.
6. Always perform when asked.
7. Remember the nobility of your purpose.

Author's Biography

Kathryn Marie Bild is a writer, acting and speaking coach, director, Grammy Award-winning video producer, and singer-songwriter. She is author of the books *Acting From A Spiritual Perspective, The Actor's Quotation Book, Einstein For Infants,* and the novels *Uncle Ethel* and *Miss Madeline Goes Shopping.* She lives in New York City.

www.kathrynmariebild.com